A cook's book
of decadence

CHOCOLATE
COFFEE
CARAMEL

whitecap

This edition first published in Canada in 2005 by Whitecap Books,
351 Lynne Ave., North Vancouver, British Columbia, Canada, V7J 2C4.
www.whitecap.ca

First published in 2005 by Murdoch Books Pty Limited.
www.murdochbooks.com.au

Design Manager: Vivien Valk
Design Concept, Design and Illustration: Alex Frampton
Editor: Gordana Trifunovic
Recipes developed by the Murdoch Books Test Kitchen
Production: Adele Troeger

ISBN 1-55285-733-6

IMPORTANT: Those who might be at risk from the effects of salmonella poisoning (the
elderly, pregnant women, young children and those suffering from immune deficiency
diseases) should consult their doctor with any concerns about eating raw eggs.

CONVERSION GUIDE: You may find cooking times vary depending on the oven you are
using. For fan-forced ovens, as a general rule, set the oven temperature 20°C (35°F) lower
than indicated in the recipe. We have used 20 ml (4 teaspoon) tablespoon measures. If you
are using a 15 ml (3 teaspoon) tablespoon, for most recipes the difference will not be
noticeable. However, for recipes using baking powder, gelatine, bicarbonate of soda (baking
soda), small amounts of flour, add an extra teaspoon for each tablespoon specified.

a cook's book

of decadence

CHOCOLATE
COFFEE
CARAMEL

Contents

a dash of indulgence

Announcing that many of the recipes in this book are familiar favourites might seem a strange thing to do. Isn't it the new and the now that we all crave? But sweet dishes — especially ones that feature chocolate, coffee and caramel — are popular precisely because they satisfy time and again. Let the savoury dish amaze! When it comes to desserts most of us seek comfort with a good dash of indulgence. The only thing that needs to amaze is our ability to eat that slice of Chocolate Mud Cake or manage one last Caramel Pecan Square when two seconds earlier we had declared not another mouthful.

Perhaps the most comforting food of all is chocolate. Smooth and rich, chocolate is the very taste of luxury. It is a treat and has always been so: the Mayans and Aztecs of Central America, where the original cacao trees grew, used the beans as a valuable object of trade, and the frothy, bitter hot drink they brewed was the preserve of the ruling class and warriors. Its introduction to the wider world and gradual refinement into the many sweet products we know today has not changed the perception of chocolate as something special. In cooking, chocolate is at the heart of sweet recipes. The following chapters contain many classics, including Double Chocolate Brownies, Chocolate Mousse and White Chocolate Roulade with Berries. Some dishes are quick and easy to make, such as

Self-saucing Chocolate Pudding, while others like Ganache Torte demand a little more effort — which can be satisfying in itself. But all lead to the same end result: yum.

A large part of chocolate's appeal in cooking is the ease with which it combines with other ingredients: spices such as cinnamon and vanilla, fruit and nuts, liqueurs, cheese and sweet breads like panettone. Coffee is another well-loved partner. Aromatic and robust, it is the perfect foil to chocolate's heady tendencies. Espresso Chocolate Cake with Liqueur Sauce and Mocha Lamingtons are just two examples of this happy balance. And if coffee offers a clean contrast to chocolate's richness, caramel is the gooey goodness in the middle. Chocolate Fudge Pudding and Caramel Slice pretty much speak for themselves. But both coffee and caramel shine in their own right in this collection. They make excellent ice creams, syrups, toppings and sauces — for starters, try Sticky Date Pudding with Caramel Sauce and Cappuccino Ice Cream Cakes. Wherever you turn in this book, delicious results await. The only unknown is whether to make the Rich Marbled Chocolate Cake or the Hazelnut Coffee Biscuits first ... or should it be the Mocha Waffles with Espresso Syrup?

Chocolate Cookies Coffee Cakes Caramel

Cakes, biscuits and slices

White Chocolate Torte Mocha Swiss Roll

Chocolate Cookies

Makes 24

125 g (4$^{1}/_{2}$ oz) dark chocolate, chopped
125 g (4$^{1}/_{2}$ oz) unsalted butter, cubed
1 egg
185 g (6$^{1}/_{2}$ oz/1 cup) soft brown sugar
185 g (6$^{1}/_{2}$ oz/1$^{1}/_{2}$ cups) self-raising flour

1 Preheat the oven to 180°C (350°F/Gas 4). Line two baking trays with baking paper.

2 Put the chocolate and butter in a heatproof bowl and set over a saucepan of simmering water. Stir occasionally until the chocolate and butter have melted.

3 Put the egg and sugar into a large bowl, and beat lightly using electric beaters for 2 minutes, or until combined. Mix in the melted chocolate. Stir in the sifted flour until just combined. Cover and refrigerate for 30 minutes, or until firm.

4 Roll tablespoons of the dough mixture into balls, then place on the prepared trays, leaving room for spreading. Press down gently with the back of a spoon. Bake for 10–12 minutes, or until firm to the touch and cracked on top. Cool on the trays for 5 minutes before transferring to a wire rack to cool completely.

Coffee Cakes

Makes 24

195 g (7 oz) unsalted butter, softened
125 g (4½ oz/²/₃ cup) soft brown sugar
2 eggs
1 tablespoon coffee and chicory essence
155 g (5½ oz/1¼ cups) self-raising flour
100 ml (3½ fl oz) buttermilk
125 g (4½ oz/1 cup) icing (confectioners') sugar

1   Preheat the oven to 150°C (300°F/Gas 2). Line two 12-hole standard muffin tins with paper cases. Beat 185 g (6½ oz) of the butter and the brown sugar using electric beaters until pale and fluffy. Add the eggs one at a time, beating well after each addition. Mix in 3 teaspoons of the coffee and chicory essence.

2   Fold the flour and a pinch of salt alternately with the buttermilk into the mixture until combined. Divide the mixture evenly among the muffin holes. Bake for 25–30 minutes, or until cakes are golden and a skewer inserted into the centre comes out clean. Leave to cool in the tray.

3   To make the icing, combine the remaining butter and essence, the icing sugar and 1½ tablespoons boiling water in a small bowl. Spread a little icing over each cake with a flat-bladed knife until evenly covered. Allow to set.

Rich Marbled Chocolate Cake

Serves 6–8

125 g (4¹/2 oz) dark chocolate, chopped
125 g (4¹/2 oz) unsalted butter
115 g (4 oz/¹/2 cup) caster (superfine) sugar
2 eggs, lightly beaten
150 g (5¹/2 oz/1¹/4 cups) self-raising flour
80 ml (2¹/2 fl oz/¹/3 cup) milk
1 tablespoon brandy
¹/2 teaspoon natural vanilla extract

CHOCOLATE ICING
100 g (3¹/2 oz) white chocolate, chopped
80 ml (2¹/2 fl oz/¹/3 cup) cream (whipping)
100 g (3¹/2 oz) dark chocolate, extra, chopped

1 Preheat the oven to 180°C (350°F/Gas 4). Lightly grease a deep 20 cm (8 inch) round cake tin and line the base and sides with baking paper.

2 Put chocolate in a heatproof bowl and set over a saucepan of simmering water. Stir until melted then remove from heat.

3 Using electric beaters, beat the butter and sugar in a large bowl until pale and fluffy. Add the eggs gradually, beating thoroughly after each addition.

4 Transfer the mixture to large bowl. Using a metal spoon, fold in the sifted flour alternately with milk. Add the brandy and vanilla extract and stir until combined. Divide the mixture in two. Add the melted chocolate to one portion and mix well.

5   Spoon the two mixtures alternately into the prepared tin. Swirl the mixture with skewer. Bake for 40 minutes, or until a skewer inserted into the centre comes out clean. Leave in the tin for 15 minutes before turning onto wire rack to cool.

6   To make the chocolate icing, put the white chocolate and 2 tablespoons of the cream in a small heatproof bowl. Set the bowl over a saucepan of simmering water, stirring until smooth. Repeat with the extra dark chocolate and remaining cream. Put alternate tablespoonfuls of mixtures on top of the cake. Swirl with a skewer to create a marbled look.

 This cake is best eaten on the day it is made.

Caramel Slice

Makes 20 pieces

125 g (4^1/$_2$ oz/1 cup) self-raising flour
90 g (3^1/$_4$ oz/1 cup) desiccated coconut
125 g (4^1/$_2$ oz/^{1}/$_2$ cup) caster (superfine) sugar
125 g (4^1/$_2$ oz) unsalted butter, melted

CARAMEL FILLING
400 g (14 oz) tin sweetened condensed milk
20 g (^{3}/$_4$ oz) unsalted butter
2 tablespoons golden or maple syrup

CHOCOLATE TOPPING
150 g (5^1/$_2$ oz) dark chocolate, chopped
20 g (^{3}/$_4$ oz) Copha (white vegetable shortening)

1   Preheat the oven to 180°C (350°F/Gas 4). Lightly grease an 18 x
    28 cm (7 x 11 inch) rectangular shallow tin and line with baking paper.

2   Sift the flour into a bowl, then mix in the coconut and sugar. Add the
    melted butter and stir well. Press firmly into the tin and bake for
    12–15 minutes, or until golden. Allow to cool.

3   To make the caramel filling, put all the ingredients in a saucepan over
    low heat. Slowly bring to the boil, stirring. Boil gently, stirring, for
    4–5 minutes, or until caramelized. Quickly pour over the cooled base,
    spreading evenly. Bake for 10 minutes, then set aside to cool.

4   To make the chocolate topping, put the ingredients in a heatproof
    bowl and set over a saucepan of simmering water. Stir until melted.
    Spread over the caramel. Refrigerate for 20 minutes, or until set.
    Cut into pieces with a hot, dry knife.

Chocolate Cake

Serves 8

125 g (4^{1}/$_{2}$ oz) unsalted butter, softened

125 g (4^{1}/$_{2}$ oz/^{1}/$_{2}$ cup) caster (superfine) sugar

40 g (1^{1}/$_{2}$ oz/^{1}/$_{3}$ cup) icing (confectioners') sugar, sifted

2 eggs, lightly beaten

1 teaspoon natural vanilla extract

80 g (2^{3}/$_{4}$ oz/^{1}/$_{4}$ cup) blackberry jam

155 g (5^{1}/$_{2}$ oz/1^{1}/$_{4}$ cups) self-raising flour

60 g (2^{1}/$_{4}$ oz/^{1}/$_{2}$ cup) unsweetened cocoa powder

1 teaspoon bicarbonate of soda (baking soda)

250 ml (9 fl oz/1 cup) milk

CHOCOLATE BUTTERCREAM

50 g (1^{3}/$_{4}$ oz) dark chocolate, finely chopped

25 g (1 oz) unsalted butter

3 teaspoons cream (whipping)

30 g (1 oz/^{1}/$_{4}$ cup) icing (confectioners') sugar, sifted

1 Preheat the oven to 180°C (350°F/Gas 4). Lightly grease a 20 cm (8 inch) square cake tin and line with baking paper.

2 Cream the butter and sugars using electric beaters until fluffy. Add the eggs, vanilla and jam. Transfer to a large bowl. Fold in the combined sifted flour, cocoa and soda alternately with the milk. Stir well.

3 Pour into the tin and bake for 45 minutes, or until a skewer inserted into the centre comes out clean. Turn out onto a wire rack to cool.

4 To make the buttercream, stir the ingredients in a saucepan over low heat until smooth and glossy. Spread over the top of the cake.

Coffee Butter Cake

Serves 18-20

310 ml (10³/4 fl oz/1¹/4 cups) buttermilk

2 tablespoons instant coffee powder

160 g (5³/4 oz) unsalted butter, softened

385 g (13¹/2 oz/1²/3 cups) light brown sugar

2 large eggs, lightly beaten

310 g (11 oz/2¹/2 cups) plain (all-purpose) flour

2¹/2 teaspoons baking powder

¹/2 teaspoon bicarbonate of soda (baking soda)

¹/4 teaspoon salt

COFFEE BUTTER CREAM

2 teaspoons instant coffee powder

185 g (6¹/2 oz) unsalted butter, softened

1 teaspoon natural vanilla extract

280 g (10 oz/2¹/4 cups) sifted icing (confectioners') sugar

1 Preheat the oven to 180°C (350°F/Gas 4). Lightly grease a 33 x 23 x 5 cm (13 x 9 x 2 inch) baking tin and line with baking paper.

2 Combine the buttermilk and 2 tablespoons of the coffee powder in a bowl. Beat the butter and the brown sugar in a large bowl using electric beaters until combined. Add the eggs gradually, beating after each addition.

3 Combine the flour, baking powder, soda and salt. Stir the flour mixture and buttermilk mixture alternately into the butter mixture. Spoon into the prepared tin and smooth the surface. Bake for 40 minutes, or until a skewer inserted into the centre comes out clean. Leave in the tin for 10 minutes then turn onto a wire rack to cool.

4 To make the coffee butter cream, dissolve the coffee powder in 1 tablespoon of hot water. Using electric beaters, mix the butter, coffee mixture and vanilla in a bowl until well combined. Gradually add the icing sugar, beating until smooth. Spread over the cake using a flat-bladed knife.

Frozen Mocha Cheesecake

Serves 10-12

115 g (4 oz) dark chocolate biscuits (cookies)
55 g (2 oz) unsalted butter, melted
unsweetened cocoa powder, for dusting

FILLING
250 g (9 oz/1 cup) ricotta cheese
225 g (8 oz) cream cheese, softened
220 g (7¾ oz/1 cup) sugar
3 eggs, separated
30 g (1 oz) instant coffee powder
115 g (4 oz) dark chocolate, melted
250 ml (9 fl oz/1 cup) cream (whipping), lightly whipped

1   Lightly grease a 25 cm (10 inch) round spring-form cake tin and line the base with baking paper. Put the biscuits in the bowl of a food processor. Process for 20 seconds, or until finely crushed. Transfer the crumbs to a bowl. Add the butter and mix well. Press firmly into the base of the tin. Refrigerate 20 minutes, or until firm.

2   To make the filling, beat the cheeses in large bowl using electric beaters until smooth. Add the sugar and beat until combined. Add the egg yolks and beat until smooth. Dissolve the coffee in 1 tablespoon of water and add to the cheese mixture with the melted chocolate. Mix well.

3   Whisk the egg whites in a clean, dry bowl until stiff peaks form. Gently fold the whipped cream then the egg whites into the cheese mixture. Pour the mixture into the tin. Cover with plastic wrap and freeze 4 hours, or until firm. Dust with sifted cocoa powder to serve.

White Chocolate Torte

Serves 10–12

3 eggs
80 g (2³/₄ oz/¹/₃ cup) caster (superfine) sugar
80 g (2³/₄ oz/¹/₂ cup) white chocolate, melted
60 g (2¹/₄ oz/¹/₂ cup) plain (all-purpose) flour

TOPPING
150 ml (5 fl oz) thickened (whipping) cream
250 g (9 oz/1²/₃ cups) white chocolate
125 g (4¹/₂ oz/²/₃ cup) mascarpone cheese

1 Preheat the oven to 180°C (350°F/Gas 4). Lightly grease a 20 cm (8 inch) spring-form cake tin.

2 Beat the eggs and sugar using electric beaters until thick and pale. Fold in the melted white chocolate and sifted flour. Pour into the prepared tin and bake for 20 minutes, or until a skewer inserted into the centre of the cake comes out clean. Set aside in the tin to cool.

3 To make the topping, put the cream and white chocolate in a saucepan. Stir constantly over low heat for 5–6 minutes, or until the chocolate has melted and the mixture is smooth. Remove from the heat and set aside to cool slightly. Stir the mascarpone into the chocolate mixture.

4 Pour the topping over the cake and refrigerate overnight, or until the topping is firm.

Triple Chocolate Cake

Serves 8–10

125 g (4¹/2 oz) unsalted butter, softened
145 g (5 oz/²/3 cup) caster (superfine) sugar
40 g (1¹/2 oz/¹/3 cup) icing (confectioners') sugar
150 g (5¹/2 oz/1¹/4 cups) self-raising flour
60 g (2¹/4 oz/¹/2 cup) unsweetened cocoa powder
1 teaspoon bicarbonate of soda (baking soda)
2 eggs, lightly beaten
250 ml (9 fl oz/1 cup) milk
1 teaspoon natural vanilla extract
60 g (2¹/4 oz/¹/3 cup) chocolate chips

ICING
115 g (4 oz/²/3 cup) chocolate chips
30 g (1 oz) unsalted butter
125 g (4¹/2 oz/1 cup) icing (confectioners') sugar

1   Preheat the oven to 180°C (350°F/Gas 4). Lightly grease a deep 19 cm (7¹/2 inch) square tin. Line the base and sides with baking paper. Beat the butter and sugars in a bowl using electric beaters until creamy.

2   Transfer the mixture to a large bowl. Add the sifted flour, cocoa and bicarbonate of soda alternately with combined eggs and milk. Beat until smooth. Using a metal spoon, fold in the extract and chocolate chips.

3   Spoon mixture into the prepared tin. Bake for 40 minutes, or until a skewer inserted into the centre comes out clean. Stand the cake in the tin for 5 minutes before turning onto a wire rack to cool.

4 To make the icing, combine the chocolate chips and the butter in a small saucepan. Stir constantly over low heat. Add the icing sugar and beat until the icing is thick. Add enough hot water to make the icing spreadable and smooth. Spread icing evenly over the cake using a palette knife.

Chocolate Chip Cookies

Makes 16

125 g (4^1/$_2$ oz) unsalted butter
185 g (6^1/$_2$ oz/1 cup) soft brown sugar
1 teaspoon natural vanilla extract
1 egg, lightly beaten
1 tablespoon milk
215 g (7^1/$_2$ oz/1^3/$_4$ cups) plain (all-purpose) flour
1 teaspoon baking powder
250 g (9 oz/1^1/$_2$ cups) dark chocolate chips

1 Preheat the oven to 180°C (350°F/Gas 4). Line a large baking tray with baking paper.

2 Cream the butter and sugar in a large bowl using electric beaters. Mix in the vanilla extract and gradually add the egg, beating well. Stir in the milk. Sift the flour and baking powder into a large bowl, then fold into the butter and egg mixture. Stir in the dark chocolate chips.

3 Drop level tablespoons of the cookie mixture onto the baking tray, leaving about 4 cm (1^1/$_2$ inches) between each cookie, then lightly press with a floured fork. Bake for 15 minutes, or until lightly golden. Cool on a wire rack.

Gâteau Tiramisu

Serves 8–10

1 tablespoon instant coffee powder

190 g (6¾ oz/¾ cup) caster (superfine) sugar

80 ml (2½ fl oz) Kahlua

4 egg yolks

500 g (1 lb 2 oz) mascarpone cheese

2 ready-made 22 cm (8½ inch) genoise sponges

300 ml (10½ fl oz) thickened (whipping) cream

unsweetened cocoa powder, for dusting

500 g (1 lb 2 oz) chocolate cream wafers (long thin cigar shapes)

1 Put the coffee and 110 g (3¾ oz) of the sugar in a saucepan with 250 ml (9 fl oz/1 cup) of water. Stir over low heat until the sugar has dissolved. Remove from the heat. Leave to cool, then add the Kahlua.

2 Beat the egg yolks and the remaining sugar in a heatproof bowl. Set the bowl over a saucepan of simmering water. Beat using electric beaters for 3 minutes, or until the mixture is thick. Remove from the heat. Transfer to a clean bowl. Beat for 3 minutes, or until cool.

3 Stir the mascarpone in a large bowl until softened. Add the egg yolk mixture, then the cream, beating slightly until thick.

4 Slice both of the cakes in half horizontally. Brush a layer of cake with the coffee syrup. Spread with about a fifth of the mascarpone cream. Top with another layer of cake. Continue layering with the syrup, cream and cake, finishing with a layer of the cream. Refrigerate the cake and remaining filling for 1 hour. Dust the top of the cake with cocoa powder. Spread the remaining cream around the side. Press the wafers side-by-side around the cake and tie with a ribbon to secure.

Cappuccino Ice Cream Cakes

Makes 10

1 tablespoon instant coffee powder
1 litre (35 fl oz/4 cups) vanilla ice cream, softened
250 ml (9 fl oz/1 cup) thick (double/heavy) cream
1 tablespoon icing (confectioners') sugar
unsweetened cocoa powder, for dusting

CHOCOLATE CAKE
185 g (6$^1/_2$ oz) unsalted butter
330 g (11$^1/_2$ oz/1$^1/_2$ cups) caster (superfine) sugar
2$^1/_2$ teaspoons natural vanilla extract
3 eggs
75 g (2$^1/_2$ oz/$^2/_3$ cup) self-raising flour
225 g (8 oz/1$^1/_4$ cups) plain (all-purpose) flour
1$^1/_2$ teaspoons bicarbonate of soda (baking soda)
90 g (3$^1/_4$ oz/$^3/_4$ cup) unsweetened cocoa powder
280 ml (9$^3/_4$ fl oz) buttermilk

1   Preheat the oven to 180°C (350°F/Gas 4). Lightly grease ten 250 ml (9 fl oz/1 cup) capacity muffin holes.

2   To make the cake, beat the butter and sugar using electric beaters until light and creamy. Beat in the vanilla extract. Add the eggs, one at a time, beating well after each addition.

3   Using a metal spoon, fold in the combined sifted flours, bicarbonate of soda and cocoa powder alternately with the buttermilk. Stir until the mixture is just combined.

4 Divide the mixture evenly among the muffin holes and bake for 25 minutes, or until a skewer inserted into the centre comes out clean. Cool in the tins for 5 minutes before turning out onto a wire cake rack to cool.

5 Dissolve the coffee powder in 2 tablespoons of boiling water, then cool. Roughly break up the vanilla ice cream in a large bowl and stir until smooth. Stir in the coffee mixture and freeze until required.

6 Beat the cream and icing sugar together in a small bowl using electric beaters until soft peaks form. Refrigerate until ready to use.

7 Cut the top off each cake, leaving a 1 cm ($\frac{1}{2}$ inch) border around the top edge of each cake and reserve the tops. Use a spoon to scoop out some of the cake, leaving a 1 cm ($\frac{1}{2}$ inch) shell of cake.

8 Soften the coffee ice cream with a spoon and pile into the cakes so it comes slightly above the top. Replace the tops and press gently. Spread cream mixture roughly over the top of each cake. Dust the tops with cocoa powder. Serve immediately.

 These cakes are best eaten on the day they are made.

Triple Chocolate Peanut Butter Cookies

Makes about 34

125 g (4^{1}/$_{2}$ oz) unsalted butter
165 g (5^{3}/$_{4}$ oz/^{3}/$_{4}$ cup) soft brown sugar
1 egg, lightly beaten
185 g (6^{1}/$_{2}$ oz/^{3}/$_{4}$ cup) peanut butter
125 g (4^{1}/$_{2}$ oz/1 cup) plain (all-purpose) flour
^{1}/$_{2}$ teaspoon bicarbonate of soda (baking soda)
30 g (1 oz/^{1}/$_{4}$ cup) unsweetened cocoa powder
175 g (6 oz/1^{1}/$_{4}$ cups) white chocolate melts (buttons)
175 g (6 oz/1^{1}/$_{4}$ cups) dark chocolate melts (buttons)

1   Preheat the oven to 180°C (350°F/Gas 4). Line two 32 x 28 cm (12^{3}/$_{4}$ x 11^{1}/$_{4}$ inch) baking trays with baking paper.

2   Using electric beaters, beat the butter and sugar in a mixing bowl until light and creamy. Add the egg gradually, beating thoroughly after each addition. Add the peanut butter and beat until combined.

3   Using a metal spoon, add the sifted flour, bicarbonate of soda and cocoa. Mix to a soft dough. Roll level tablespoons of mixture into balls. Place on the prepared trays and flatten with a fork in a criss-cross pattern. Bake for 20 minutes. Cool on the trays for 5 minutes before transferring to wire racks. Allow biscuits to cool completely.

4   Put the white chocolate melts in a small heatproof bowl and set over a saucepan of simmering water. Stir until the chocolate is melted and smooth. Dip one-third of each cookie in the white chocolate. Place on a wire rack to set. Melt the dark chocolate melts in the same way, and dip the opposite one-third of each cookie, leaving a plain band in the centre.

Baked Chocolate Cheesecake

serves 8–10

125 g (4¹/₂ oz) plain chocolate biscuits (cookies)
40 g (1¹/₂ oz/¹/₄ cup) chopped almonds
90 g (3¹/₄ oz) unsalted butter, melted
1 tablespoon soft brown sugar

FILLING
500 g (1 lb 2 oz) cream cheese, at room temperature
95 g (3¹/₄ oz/¹/₂ cup) soft brown sugar
125 g (4¹/₂ oz) dark chocolate, melted
125 ml (4 fl oz/¹/₂ cup) thickened (whipping) cream
2 eggs, beaten
1 teaspoon grated orange zest

1   Lightly grease a 20 cm (8 inch) round spring-form cake tin and
    line the base with baking paper. Put the biscuits in a food processor
    with the almonds and process into crumbs. Add the butter and
    sugar and process again until well combined. Press firmly into the
    base of the tin and refrigerate until firm. Preheat the oven to 160°C
    (315°F/Gas 2–3).

2   To make the filling, beat the cream cheese and sugar together until
    the mixture is creamy. Blend in the melted chocolate, cream, eggs
    and orange zest and mix until smooth. Pour the filling over the crumb
    crust and smooth the surface. Bake for 1 hour 20 minutes, or until
    the filling is firm to the touch.

3   Leave the cheesecake to cool in the tin and refrigerate overnight.

White Chocolate Roulade with Berries

Serves 6-8

ROULADE

4 eggs, separated

115 g (4 oz/$^1/_2$ cup) caster (superfine) sugar, plus extra, for sprinkling

60 g (2$^1/_4$ oz/$^1/_2$ cup) finely grated white chocolate

60 g (2$^1/_4$ oz/$^1/_2$ cup) self-raising flour

100 g (3$^1/_2$ oz/$^2/_3$ cup) strawberries, sliced

100 g (3$^1/_2$ oz/$^3/_4$ cup) fresh raspberries

1–2 tablespoons caster (superfine) sugar, to taste

185 ml (6 fl oz/$^3/_4$ cup) thickened (whipping) cream

2 teaspoons icing (confectioners') sugar, plus extra, for dusting

1 teaspoon natural vanilla extract

1 Preheat the oven to 200°C (400°F/Gas 6). Lightly grease a 25 x 30 cm (10 x 12 inch) Swiss roll tin (jelly roll tin) and line with baking paper, overlapping the two long sides.

2 Beat the egg yolks and sugar using electric beaters for 5 minutes, or until thick and creamy. Fold in 1 tablespoon of hot water and the white chocolate. Sift the flour over the mixture and fold through until combined.

3 Beat the egg whites using electric beaters until soft peaks form. Using a large metal spoon, fold the egg whites through the chocolate mixture until just combined. Pour the mixture into the prepared tin. Bake for 10–12 minutes, or until golden brown and firm to the touch.

4 Put a large sheet of baking paper on a flat surface and sprinkle with caster sugar. Turn the roulade out onto the sugared paper. Trim the crisp edges and roll up from the short end with the aid of the baking paper. Set aside for 5 minutes, then unroll and leave to cool.

5 Meanwhile, put the berries in a bowl and sweeten with caster sugar, to taste. Beat the cream, icing sugar and vanilla until firm peaks form. Spread the roulade with the cream and sprinkle the berries over the top. Roll up and dust with icing sugar. Cut into slices to serve.

Hazelnut Coffee Biscuits

Makes 50-60

125 g (4^1/$_2$ oz) unsalted butter

115 g (4 oz/^{1}/$_2$ cup) caster (superfine) sugar

1 teaspoon grated lemon zest

1 egg yolk

1 teaspoon lemon juice

125 g (4^1/$_2$ oz/1 cup) ground hazelnuts

155 g (5^1/$_2$ oz/1^1/$_4$ cups) plain (all-purpose) flour

COFFEE CREAM

110 g (3^3/$_4$ oz/^{1}/$_2$ cup) sugar

1 tablespoon instant coffee powder

80 g (2^2/$_3$ oz) unsalted butter

1 Preheat the oven to 180°C (350°F/Gas 4). Line two baking trays with baking paper.

2 Beat the butter and sugar using electric beaters until creamy. Add the zest, egg yolk, juice and nuts and beat well. Stir in the flour. Form the mixture into a ball. Wrap in plastic wrap. Refrigerate for 20 minutes. Divide the mixture in half. Roll one portion between two sheets of baking paper to a thickness of 4 mm (^{1}/$_4$ inch). Cut out rounds using a 3 cm (1^1/$_4$ inch) fluted cutter. Put the rounds on the trays. Repeat with the remaining dough. Bake for 10 minutes, or until golden.

3 To make the coffee cream, combine the sugar, 60 ml (2 fl oz/^{1}/$_4$ cup) of water, and the coffee in a saucepan. Bring to the boil. Simmer for 5 minutes. Beat the butter until creamy. Combine the cooled syrup and the butter, beating until thick. Put into a paper piping bag, snip off the tip to form an inverted 'v' and pipe rosettes onto each biscuit.

Pecan and Coffee Biscotti

Makes 40

215 g (7^1/$_2$ oz/1^3/$_4$ cups) plain (all-purpose) flour

^{1}/$_2$ teaspoon baking powder

160 g (5^3/$_4$ oz/^{2}/$_3$ cup) caster (superfine) sugar, plus extra for sprinkling

60 g (2^1/$_4$ oz) unsalted butter

2 eggs

^{1}/$_2$ teaspoon natural vanilla extract

40 g (1^1/$_2$ oz) instant coffee powder

135 g (4^3/$_4$ oz/1^1/$_3$ cups) pecans

1 Preheat the oven to 180°C (350°F/Gas 4). Line two baking trays with baking paper. Put the sifted flour, baking powder, sugar and a pinch of salt in a food processor and mix for 1–2 seconds. Add the butter and mix until the mixture resembles fine breadcrumbs. Add the eggs and vanilla and process until smooth.

2 Transfer the dough to a floured surface and knead in the coffee and pecans. Divide into two equal portions and, using lightly floured hands, shape each into a log about 20 cm (8 inches) long. Put the logs on the baking trays and sprinkle with the extra caster sugar. Press the top of each log down gently to make an oval.

3 Bake for 35 minutes, or until golden. Set aside to cool for about 20 minutes. Reduce the oven to 170°C (325°F/Gas 3).

4 Cut the logs into 1 cm (^{1}/$_2$ inch) slices. Turn the baking paper over, then spread the biscotti apart on the tray so that they do not touch. Return to the oven and bake for 30 minutes, or until they just begin to colour. Cool completely before storing in an airtight container.

Sacher Torte

125 g (4^1/$_2$ oz/1 cup) plain (all-purpose) flour

30 g (1 oz/^{1}/$_4$ cup) unsweetened cocoa powder

250 g (9 oz/1 cup) caster (superfine) sugar

100 g (3^1/$_2$ oz) unsalted butter

80 g (2^3/$_4$ oz/^{1}/$_4$ cup) strawberry jam

4 eggs, separated

GANACHE TOPPING

170 ml (5^1/$_2$ fl oz/^{2}/$_3$ cup) cream (whipping)

90 g (3 oz/^{1}/$_3$ cup) caster (superfine) sugar

200 g (7 oz) dark chocolate, chopped

1 Preheat the oven to 180°C (350°F/Gas 4). Lightly grease a 20 cm (8 inch) round cake tin and line with baking paper.

2 Sift the flour and cocoa into a bowl and make a well. Combine the sugar, butter and half the jam in a saucepan. Stir over low heat until the butter is melted and the sugar has dissolved. Add to the flour with the lightly beaten egg yolks and stir until just combined.

3 Beat the egg whites in a bowl using electric beaters until soft peaks form. Stir a third of the egg white into the cake mixture, then fold in the rest in two batches. Pour into the tin and smooth the surface. Bake for 40–45 minutes, or until a skewer inserted into the centre comes out clean. Leave in the tin for 15 minutes before turning out onto a wire rack to cool.

4 To make the topping, stir the cream, sugar and chocolate in a saucepan over low heat until the mixture is melted and smooth.

5 Trim the top of the cake so that it is flat, then turn it upside down on a wire rack over a tray. Melt the remaining jam and brush it over the cake. Pour most of the topping over the cake and tap the tray to flatten the surface. Traditionally, the word 'Sacher' is piped in chocolate across the top of the cake.

Chocolate Truffle Macaroon Slice

Makes 24 pieces

3 egg whites
185 g (6^1/$_2$ oz/^{3}/$_4$ cup) caster (superfine) sugar
180 g (6^1/$_4$ oz/2 cups) desiccated coconut
250 g (9 oz) dark chocolate, chopped
300 ml (10^1/$_2$ fl oz) cream (whipping)
1 tablespoon unsweetened cocoa powder, for dusting

1   Preheat the oven to 180°C (350°F/Gas 4). Lightly grease a 20 x 30 cm (8 x 12 inch) shallow baking tin and line with baking paper, leaving it hanging over the two long sides.

2   Beat the egg whites in a clean, dry bowl until soft peaks form. Slowly add the sugar, beating well after each addition until stiff and glossy. Fold in the coconut. Spread into the tin and bake for 20 minutes, or until light brown. While still warm, press down lightly but firmly with a palette knife. Cool completely.

3   Put the chocolate in a heatproof bowl and set over a saucepan of simmering water. Stir occasionally until the chocolate has melted. Cool slightly.

4   Beat the cream until thick. Gently fold in the chocolate until well combined. Spread evenly over the base and refrigerate for 3 hours, or until set. Lift from the tin and dust with the cocoa.

Chocolate and Almond Torte

Serves 8–10

150 g (5^1/$_2$ oz) flaked or whole almonds

1 slice pandoro or 1 small brioche

300 g (10^1/$_2$ oz) dark chocolate

2 tablespoons brandy

150 g (5^1/$_2$ oz) unsalted butter, softened

150 g (5^1/$_2$ oz/^{2}/$_3$ cup) caster (superfine) sugar

4 eggs

1 teaspoon natural vanilla extract

200 g (7 oz) mascarpone cheese

crème fraîche, to serve

unsweetened cocoa powder, for dusting

1   Preheat the oven to 170°C (325°F/Gas 4). Toast the almonds in the oven for 3–4 minutes, or until golden brown.

2   Put the almonds and pandoro in a food processor and process until the mixture resembles coarse breadcrumbs. Lightly grease a 23 cm (9 inch) spring-form cake tin. Tip some of the mixture into the tin and shake so that it forms a coating on the bottom and side.

3   Put the chocolate and brandy in a heatproof bowl and set over a saucepan of simmering water. Stir occasionally until melted.

4   Cream the butter and sugar in the food processor for a few minutes until light and pale. Add the melted chocolate, eggs, vanilla and mascarpone. Add the remaining nut mixture and mix well. Tip into the tin. Bake for 50–60 minutes, or until just set. Leave to rest in the tin for about 15 minutes before taking out. When cool, dust with a little cocoa powder and serve with crème fraîche, if desired.

Chocolate Spice Cake

Serves 8

60 g (2^{1}/$_{4}$ oz) unsalted butter, softened
165 g (5^{3}/$_{4}$ oz/^{3}/$_{4}$ cup) sugar
2 large eggs, lightly beaten
3 tablespoons dark corn syrup
155 g (5^{1}/$_{2}$ oz/1^{1}/$_{4}$ cups) plain (all-purpose) flour
30 g (1 oz/^{1}/$_{4}$ cup) unsweetened cocoa powder
1^{1}/$_{4}$ teaspoons baking powder
^{1}/$_{4}$ teaspoon bicarbonate of soda (baking soda)
^{1}/$_{4}$ teaspoon salt
^{1}/$_{4}$ teaspoon ground cloves
^{1}/$_{4}$ teaspoon ground allspice
170 ml (5^{1}/$_{2}$ fl oz/^{2}/$_{3}$ cup) milk

SPICY SYRUP
110 g (3^{3}/$_{4}$ oz/^{1}/$_{2}$ cup) sugar
^{1}/$_{4}$ teaspoon ground cloves
^{1}/$_{4}$ teaspoon ground allspice

1 Preheat the oven to 180°C (350°F/Gas 4). Lightly grease a 20 cm (8 inch) round cake tin and line with baking paper.

2 Beat the butter and sugar in small mixing bowl using electric beaters until pale and fluffy. Add the eggs gradually, beating thoroughly after each addition. Add the dark corn syrup and beat until combined.

3 Sift together the flour, cocoa powder, baking powder, soda, salt, ^{1}/$_{4}$ teaspoon cloves and ^{1}/$_{4}$ teaspoon allspice onto waxed paper. Stir the flour mixture and milk alternately into the butter mixture.

Stir until mixture is almost smooth. Spoon the mixture into the prepared tin and smooth the surface. Bake for 45 minutes, or until a skewer inserted into the centre comes out clean. Leave the cake in the tin and put on a wire rack to cool.

4 To make the spicy syrup, combine 170 ml (5½ fl oz/⅔ cup) water, sugar, cloves and allspice in small saucepan. Stir constantly over high heat until the mixture boils and the sugar is dissolved. Reduce the heat and boil gently, uncovered, for about 15 minutes or until mixture is reduced by half, stirring occasionally. Remove from heat and allow to cool slightly.

5 Pour the hot spicy syrup over the cake while it is still in the tin. When all the syrup has been absorbed, remove the cake from the tin.

This cake is best eaten the day it is made.

Double Chocolate Brownies

Makes 12

80 g (2^3/4 oz) unsalted butter, melted
40 g (1^1/2 oz/^{1}/3 cup) unsweetened cocoa powder
145 g (5 oz/^{2}/3 cup) caster (superfine) sugar
2 eggs
60 g (2^1/4 oz/^{1}/2 cup) plain (all-purpose) flour
^{1}/2 teaspoon baking powder
100 g (3^1/2 oz/^{1}/2 cup) chocolate chips

1 Preheat the oven to 180°C (350°F/Gas 4). Lightly grease a 23 cm (9 inch) square shallow tin and line the base with baking paper.

2 Combine the melted butter, cocoa and sugar, followed by the eggs. Sift in the flour and baking powder, along with a pinch of salt, then mix well. Make sure you don't have any pockets of flour. Add the chocolate chips and stir to combine.

3 Pour the mixture into the prepared tin and bake for 30 minutes, or until just firm to the touch. Allow to cool in the tin, then cut into pieces.

High-top Cappuccino and White-choc Muffins

Makes 8

20 g (^{3}/4 oz/^{1}/4 cup) instant coffee powder

310 g (11 oz/2^1/2 cups) self-raising flour

115 g (4 oz/^{1}/2 cup) caster (superfine) sugar

2 eggs, lightly beaten

375 ml (13 fl oz/1^1/2 cups) buttermilk

1 teaspoon natural vanilla extract

180 g (6^1/2 oz) unsalted butter, melted

100 g (3^1/2 oz) white chocolate, roughly chopped

60 g (2^1/4 oz/^{1}/3 cup) soft brown sugar

1   Preheat the oven to 200°C (400°F/Gas 6). Cut eight lengths of baking paper and roll into 8 cm (3^1/4 inch) high cylinders to fit into eight 125 ml (4 fl oz/^{1}/2 cup) capacity ramekins. When in place in the ramekins, secure the cylinders with string and put all the ramekins onto a baking tray.

2   Dissolve the coffee in 1 tablespoon of boiling water and allow to cool. Sift the flour and sugar into a bowl. Combine the egg, buttermilk, vanilla, 150 g (5^1/2 oz) of the melted butter, the white chocolate and coffee mixture and combine with the dry ingredients. Spoon the mixture into each cylinder.

3   Heat the remaining butter and the brown sugar and stir until the sugar dissolves. Spoon the mixture onto each muffin and gently swirl into the muffin using a skewer. Bake for 25–30 minutes, or until a skewer inserted into the centre of a muffin comes out clean.

Mocha Swiss Roll

Serves 6-8

3 egg whites

115 g (4 oz/^{1}/2 cup) caster (superfine) sugar

3 egg yolks, lightly beaten

2 tablespoons hot milk

140 g (5 oz) plain (all-purpose) flour

40 g (1^1/2 oz/^{1}/3 cup) unsweetened cocoa powder

3 teaspoons instant coffee powder

2 teaspoons baking powder

1 tablespoon caster (superfine) sugar, extra

250 ml (9 fl oz/1 cup) cream (whipping)

55 g (2 oz) chocolate bar, crumbled

45 g (1^1/2 oz/^{1}/2 cup) flaked almonds

1 Preheat the oven to 220°C (425°F/Gas 7). Lightly grease a shallow 30 x 25 cm (12 x 10 inch) Swiss roll tin (jelly roll tin) and line the base and two sides with baking paper.

2 Beat the egg whites in a bowl using electric beaters until soft peaks form. Add the sugar gradually, beating until the mixture is thick and all the sugar is dissolved. Add the beaten egg yolks. Beat for a further 20 seconds. Transfer the mixture to a large bowl. Fold in the milk, flour, cocoa, coffee and baking powder.

3 Spread the mixture evenly in the prepared tin and smooth the surface. Bake for 8 minutes, or until springy to the touch.

4 Sprinkle a large sheet of baking paper with the extra sugar. Turn the cake onto the paper and allow to stand for 1 minute. Trim the ends of the roll with a serrated knife. Carefully roll the cake up with the baking paper. Stand the cake for 5 minutes, or until cool.

5 Whip the cream with the extra coffee powder. Fold through half the crumbled chocolate and all the flaked almonds. Unroll the cake, spread with most of the cream mixture, then re-roll using the baking paper as a guide. Put the cake on a serving plate. Decorate with the remaining cream and crumbled chocolate to serve.

 This cake is best eaten on the day it is made.

Coffee and Brazil Nut Biscotti

Makes 40 pieces

3 teaspoons instant coffee powder

1 tablespoon dark rum, warmed

2 eggs

125 g (4^1/$_2$ oz/^{1}/$_2$ cup) caster (superfine) sugar

155 g (5^1/$_2$ oz/1^1/$_4$ cups) plain (all-purpose) flour

60 g (2^1/$_4$ oz/^{1}/$_2$ cup) self-raising flour

1 teaspoon ground cinnamon

105 g (3^1/$_2$ oz/^{3}/$_4$ cup) brazil nuts, roughly chopped

1 tablespoon caster (superfine) sugar, extra

1. Preheat the oven to 180°C (350°F/Gas 4). Dissolve the coffee in the rum. Beat the eggs and sugar until thick and creamy, then beat in the coffee. Sift the flours and cinnamon into a bowl, then stir in the nuts. Mix in the coffee mixture.

2. Divide the mixture into two rolls, each about 28 cm (11 inches) long. Line a baking tray with baking paper, put the rolls on it and press lightly to flatten to about 6 cm (2^1/$_2$ inches) across. Brush lightly with water and sprinkle with the extra sugar. Bake for 25 minutes, or until firm and light brown. Cool until warm on the tray. Reduce the oven temperature to 160°C (315°F/Gas 2–3).

3. Cut into 1 cm (^{1}/$_2$ inch) thick diagonal slices. Bake in a single layer on the lined tray for 20 minutes, or until dry, turning once. Cool on a rack.

 Store in an airtight container for 2–3 weeks.

Sour Cream Coffee Cake

Serves 10-12

125 g (4¹/₂ oz) unsalted butter, softened

250 g (9 oz/1 cup) caster (superfine) sugar

3 eggs, lightly beaten

1 teaspoon natural vanilla extract

1 tablespoon instant coffee powder

90 g (3¹/₄ oz/³/₄ cup) plain (all-purpose) flour

60 g (2¹/₄ oz/¹/₂ cup) self-raising flour

90 g (3¹/₄ oz/¹/₃ cup) sour cream

COFFEE ICING

2 teaspoons instant coffee powder

125 g (4¹/₂ oz/1 cup) icing (confectioners') sugar

20 g (³/₄ oz) unsalted butter, melted

1 Preheat the oven to 160°C (315°F/Gas 2–3). Lightly grease a shallow 28 x 18 cm (11 x 7 inch) cake tin and line with baking paper.

2 Cream the butter and sugar in a bowl using electric beaters. Add the egg gradually, beating after each addition. Dissolve the vanilla and coffee powder in 1 tablespoon of warm water and beat into the mixture. Transfer to a large bowl. Fold in the sifted flours alternately with the sour cream. Stir until the mixture is just combined.

3 Spoon the mixture into the tin and bake for 30–40 minutes, or until a skewer inserted into the centre comes out clean. Allow to cool in the tin for 5 minutes before turning out onto a wire rack to cool.

4 To make the icing, dissolve the coffee in 1 tablespoon warm water. Add the icing sugar and butter and mix well. Spread over the cake.

Caramel Cream Cake

Serves 12-16

185 g (6^1/$_2$ oz) unsalted butter, softened

285 g (10 oz/1^1/$_4$ cups) light brown sugar

2 large eggs, lightly beaten

60 ml (2 fl oz/^{1}/$_4$ cup) dark corn syrup

1 teaspoon natural vanilla extract

310 g (11 oz/1^1/$_2$ cups) plain (all-purpose) flour

1 tablespoon baking powder

^{1}/$_4$ teaspoon bicarbonate of soda (baking soda)

^{1}/$_4$ teaspoon salt

250 ml (9 fl oz/1 cup) milk

40 g (1^1/$_2$ oz/^{1}/$_3$ cup) slivered almonds, toasted

CARAMEL CREAM

250 ml (9 fl oz/1 cup) thickened (whipping) cream

40 g (1^1/$_2$ oz) firmly packed light brown sugar

1 teaspoon natural vanilla extract

1 Preheat the oven to 180°C (350°F/Gas 4). Lightly grease two 20 cm (8 inch) round cake tins and line with baking paper.

2 Cream the butter and brown sugar in small bowl using electric beaters until pale and fluffy. Add the beaten eggs gradually, beating after each addition.

3 Add the corn syrup and vanilla and beat until combined. Transfer the mixture to large bowl. Sift together the flour, baking powder, soda and salt. Stir the flour mixture and milk alternately into the butter mix. Stir just until combined and almost smooth.

4   Divide between the prepared tins and smooth the surface. Bake for 40–45 minutes, or until a skewer inserted into the centre comes out clean. Leave the cakes in the tins for 10 minutes before turning out onto wire racks to cool.

5   To make the caramel cream, whip the cream to soft peaks. Add the brown sugar and vanilla. Continue whipping to stiff peaks.

6   Place one of the cakes on a serving plate and spread with half the cream mixture. Cover with the second cake. Spread the remaining cream over the top and sprinkle with the toasted almonds.

White Chocolate Cheesecakes with Mixed Berries

Serves 4

4 butternut biscuits (cookies)
75 g (2¹/2 oz/¹/2 cup) white chocolate chips
250 g (9 oz) cream cheese, at room temperature
60 ml (2 fl oz/¹/4 cup) cream (whipping)
125 g (4¹/2 oz/¹/2 cup) caster (superfine) sugar
1 egg
250 g (9 oz) mixed berries, such as raspberries, blueberries
   and sliced strawberries
Framboise or Cointreau (optional), to flavour

1   Preheat the oven to 160°C (315°F/Gas 2–3). Lightly grease four
    250 ml (9 fl oz/1 cup) muffin holes. Line with 2 strips of baking paper
    to make a cross pattern. Put a biscuit in the base of each hole. Put
    the chocolate chips in a heatproof bowl and set over a saucepan of
    simmering water. Stir occasionally until the chocolate has melted.

2   Using electric beaters, beat the cream cheese, cream and half the
    sugar until thick and smooth. Beat in the egg and then the melted
    chocolate. Divide the mixture among the muffin holes. Bake for
    25 minutes, or until set. Cool in the tin then run a small spatula
    around the edge and lift out of the holes with the paper strips.
    Refrigerate for 1 hour, or until ready to serve.

3   Put the berries in a bowl and fold in the remaining sugar. Leave for
    10–15 minutes, or until juices form. Flavour with a little liqueur, such
    as Framboise or Cointreau, if desired. Serve the cheesecakes on
    individual plates topped with the berries.

Cappuccino Brownies

Serves 6

150 g (5¹/2 oz) unsalted butter
125 g (4¹/2 oz) dark chocolate
3 eggs
375 g (13 oz/1²/3 cups) caster (superfine) sugar
1 teaspoon natural vanilla extract
125 g (4¹/2 oz/1 cup) plain (all-purpose) flour
30 g (1 oz/¹/4 cup) unsweetened cocoa powder
2 tablespoons instant coffee powder
1 litre (35 fl oz/4 cups) vanilla ice cream
sweetened cocoa powder, for dusting

1   Preheat the oven to 180°C (350°F/Gas 4). Lightly grease a 28 x 18 cm (11 x 7 inch) shallow baking tin and line the base with baking paper, extending over two sides.

2   Put the butter and chocolate in a small heatproof bowl and set over a saucepan of simmering water. Stir until melted and smooth. Allow to cool slightly.

3   In a large bowl, whisk the eggs, sugar and vanilla together. Whisk in the chocolate mixture, then stir in the sifted flour, cocoa and coffee powder. Pour into the tin and bake for 40 minutes. Cool in the tin until warm.

4   Lift the brownie from the tin using the baking paper. Using an 8 cm (3 inch) round biscuit (cookie) cutter, cut out 6 rounds while the brownie is still warm. Put each round on a serving plate, top with 3 small scoops of ice cream and dust lightly with cocoa powder. Serve immediately.

Liqueur Coffee Cheesecake

serves 6-8

150 g (5¹/2 oz) ginger nut biscuits (ginger snap), finely crushed

80 g (2³/4 oz/³/4 cup) ground hazelnuts

100 g (3¹/2 oz) unsalted butter, melted

400 g (14 oz) cream cheese, softened

60 g (2¹/4 oz/¹/4 cup) sugar

3 eggs

30 g (1 oz) plain (all-purpose) flour

125 ml (4 fl oz/¹/2 cup) cream (whipping)

80 ml (2¹/2 fl oz/¹/3 cup) Kahlua, Tia Maria or Bailey's Irish Cream

TOPPING

375 g (13 oz/1¹/2 cups) sugar

1 teaspoon instant coffee powder

100 g (3¹/2 oz/³/4 cup) whole roasted hazelnuts

315 ml (10³/4 fl oz/1¹/4 cups) cream (whipping)

1 Lightly grease a 20 cm (8 inch) round spring-form cake tin and line the base with baking paper.

2 Combine the biscuits, hazelnuts and butter. Press half of the mixture firmly into the base of the tin. Gradually press the remainder around the side. Refrigerate for 10–15 minutes.

3 Preheat the oven to 180°C (350°F/Gas 4). Beat the cream cheese and sugar using electric beaters until smooth. Add the eggs one at a time, beating well after each addition. Blend together the flour and cream, and beat into the cream cheese mixture, then add the liqueur. Pour into the prepared tin and bake for 40–50 minutes, or until almost set. Set aside until completely set. Refrigerate for several hours.

4 To make the topping, combine the sugar in a pan with 185 ml (6 fl oz/$^3/_4$ cup) of water. Stir over low heat without boiling until the sugar has dissolved. Simmer for 10–12 minutes, or until golden. Remove from the heat and gently stir in the coffee. Using two spoons, dip the nuts one at a time into the toffee and put on a lightly oiled foil-lined baking tray. Allow to set. Whip the cream to firm peaks. Ease the cheesecake out of the tin and top with whipped cream and toffee hazelnuts.

Caramel Brownies

Makes 16

60 g (2^1/$_4$ oz/^{1}/$_2$ cup) self-raising flour

40 g (1^1/$_2$ oz/^{1}/$_3$ cup) plain (all-purpose) flour

150 g (5^1/$_2$ oz) unsalted butter, softened

230 g (8^1/$_2$ oz/1^1/$_4$ cups) soft brown sugar, plus extra, for sprinkling

2 eggs

1 tablespoon milk

1 teaspoon natural vanilla extract

75 g (2^1/$_2$ oz/^{3}/$_4$ cup) walnut halves, chopped

1 Preheat the oven to 180°C (350°F/Gas 4). Lightly grease a 20 cm (8 inch) square tin and line the base with baking paper.

2 Sift the flours together into a bowl. In a large bowl, beat the butter and the sugar until light and creamy. Add 1 egg, beat well and add 1 tablespoon of the flour mixture. Beat in the second egg, milk and vanilla. Fold in the remaining flour and 50 g (1^3/$_4$ oz/^{1}/$_2$ cup) walnuts. Spoon into the tin and smooth the surface.

3 Scatter the top with the remaining chopped walnuts and extra brown sugar. Bake for 35–40 minutes. Allow to cool in the tin. Carefully turn out and cut into squares.

Chocolate Swiss Roll

serves 6–8

3 eggs
125 g (4^1/$_2$ oz/^{1}/$_2$ cup) caster (superfine) sugar
30 g (1 oz/^{1}/$_4$ cup) plain (all-purpose) flour
2 tablespoons unsweetened cocoa powder
250 ml (9 fl oz/1 cup) cream (whipping)
1 tablespoon icing (confectioners') sugar, plus extra, for dusting
^{1}/$_2$ teaspoon natural vanilla extract

1   Preheat the oven to 200°C (400°F/Gas 6). Lightly grease a 30 x 25 cm (12 x 10 inch) Swiss roll tin (jelly roll tin). Line the base with baking paper, leaving the paper hanging over the two long sides.

2   Beat the eggs and 90 g (3 oz/^{1}/$_3$ cup) of the caster sugar in a bowl using electric beaters until thick and creamy. Using a metal spoon, gently fold in the combined sifted flour and cocoa.

3   Spread the mixture into the tin and smooth the surface. Bake for 10–12 minutes, or until the cake is just set. Meanwhile, put a clean tea towel (dish towel) on the work surface, cover with baking paper and sprinkle with the remaining caster sugar. When the cake is cooked, turn it out onto the sugar. Roll the cake up from the short side, rolling the paper inside the roll and using the tea towel as a guide. Stand the rolled cake on a wire rack for 5 minutes, then unroll and allow the cake to cool to room temperature. Trim the ends.

4   Beat the cream, icing sugar and vanilla until stiff peaks form. Spread the cream over the cooled cake. Re-roll the cake, using the paper as a guide. Put the roll, seam-side down, on a tray. Refrigerate, covered, for 30 minutes. Dust the top with icing sugar. Cut into slices to serve.

White Chocolate and Yoghurt Cake

Serves 8–10

90 g (3^{1}/4 oz) unsalted butter, softened
165 g (5^{3}/4 oz/^{3}/4 cup) sugar
2 large eggs, lightly beaten
1 teaspoon natural vanilla extract
60 g (2^{1}/4 oz) white chocolate, coarsely chopped
155 g (5^{1}/2 oz/1^{1}/4 cups) plain (all-purpose) flour
1^{3}/4 teaspoons baking powder
^{1}/4 teaspoon salt
125 g (4^{1}/2 oz/^{1}/2 cup) vanilla yoghurt
60 ml (2 fl oz/^{1}/4 cup) milk

WHITE CHOCOLATE TOPPING
175 g (6 oz) cream cheese, softened
85 g (3 oz) white chocolate, melted
60 g (2^{1}/4 oz/^{1}/4 cup) sugar
60 g (2^{1}/4 oz/^{1}/4 cup) vanilla yoghurt

1   Preheat the oven to 180°C (350°F/Gas 4). Lightly grease a 23 cm
(9 inch) round cake tin and line with baking paper. Beat the butter
and sugar in a small bowl using electric beaters until pale and fluffy.
Add the eggs gradually. Beat well after each addition. Add the vanilla
extract and beat until combined.

2   Put the white chocolate in a heatproof bowl and set over a saucepan
of simmering water. Stir until melted, then remove from the heat.
Combine the flour, baking powder and salt. Stir the melted white
chocolate and yoghurt into the butter mixture. Stir the flour mixture
and milk alternately into the yoghurt mixture until almost smooth.

3 Spoon into the prepared tin and smooth the surface. Bake for
   35 minutes, or until a skewer inserted into the centre comes out
   clean. Leave for 10 minutes then turn out onto a wire rack to cool.

4 To make the white chocolate topping, beat the cream cheese until
   light and creamy. Add the melted white chocolate, sugar and vanilla
   yoghurt and beat until smooth and fluffy. Spread the icing over the
   top of the cake using a flat-bladed knife.

Chocolate Chip Cake

Serves 12

160 g (5³/4 oz) unsalted butter, softened

220 g (7³/4 oz/1 cup) granulated sugar

4 large eggs, lightly beaten

1 teaspoon natural vanilla extract

300 g (10¹/2 oz/2 cups) milk chocolate chips

375 g (13 oz/3 cups) plain (all-purpose) flour

1 tablespoon baking powder

³/4 teaspoon baking soda

¹/4 teaspoon salt

170 ml (5¹/2 fl oz/²/3 cup) milk

MILK CHOCOLATE ICING

40 g (1¹/2 oz) unsalted butter

2 tablespoons thickened (whipped) cream

1 tablespoon icing (confectioners') sugar

75 g (2¹/2 oz/¹/2 cup) milk chocolate melts (buttons)

1 Preheat the oven to 180°C (350°F/Gas 4). Lightly grease a 3 litre (104 fl oz/12-cup) fluted tube tin. Coat the tin with flour and shake off any excess. Beat the butter and sugar in a bowl using electric beaters until pale and fluffy. Gradually add the eggs and beat after each addition. Add the vanilla and beat until combined.

2 Put 100 g (3¹/2 oz/²/3 cup) of the chocolate chips in a heatproof bowl and set over a saucepan of simmering water. Stir until the chocolate has melted. Transfer the butter mixture to a large bowl. Stir in the melted chocolate. Allow to cool slightly. Add the remaining chocolate chips.

3   Combine the flour, baking powder, soda and salt. Stir the flour mixture and milk alternately into the butter mixture. Stir until the mixture is almost smooth. Spoon the mixture into the prepared tin and smooth the surface. Bake for 55 minutes, or until a skewer inserted into the centre comes out clean. Allow to cool in the tin for 10 minutes before turning out onto a wire rack to cool.

4   To make the icing, melt the butter in a small saucepan. Add the cream, icing sugar and the chocolate melts, Stir over low heat until the chocolate melts and the mixture is smooth. Remove from the heat. Cool slightly. Drizzle the icing over the cake.

Chocolate Muffins

Makes 12

310 g (11 oz/2^1/$_2$ cups) self-raising flour

40 g (1^1/$_2$ oz/^{1}/$_3$ cup) unsweetened cocoa powder

^{1}/$_2$ teaspoon bicarbonate of soda (baking soda)

180 g (6 oz/^{3}/$_4$ cup) caster (superfine) sugar

375 ml (13 fl oz/1^1/$_2$ cups) buttermilk

2 eggs

150 g (5^1/$_2$ oz) unsalted butter, melted and cooled

1 Preheat the oven to 200°C (400°F/Gas 6). Lightly grease a 12-hole standard muffin tin. Sift the flour, cocoa powder and bicarbonate of soda into a bowl and add the sugar. Make a well in the centre.

2 In a jug, whisk the buttermilk and eggs together and pour into the well. Add the butter and fold gently with a metal spoon until just combined. Do not overmix — the mixture should still be lumpy.

3 Fill each hole about three-quarters full. Bake for 20–25 minutes, or until the muffins are risen and come away slightly from the side of the tin. Allow to cool for a couple of minutes, then loosen with a flat-bladed knife and transfer to a wire rack to cool.

Layered Caramel Banana Cake

Serves 8–10

90 g (3 1/4 oz/1/3 cup) unsalted butter, softened

220 g (7 3/4 oz/1 cup) sugar

1 large egg, lightly beaten

300 g (10 1/2 oz/1 1/4 cups) mashed banana (about 3 bananas)

310 g (11 oz/2 1/2 cups) plain (all-purpose) flour

1 tablespoon baking powder

1/4 teaspoon salt

60 ml (2 fl oz/1/4 cup) milk

60 g (2 1/4 oz/1/2 cup) slivered almonds

80 ml (2 1/2 fl oz/1/3 cup) dark corn syrup

1/2 teaspoon ground cinnamon

sifted icing (confectioners') sugar, for dusting

1 Preheat the oven to 180°C (350°F/Gas 4). Lightly grease a 20 cm (8 inch) round spring-form cake tin. Line with baking paper. Beat the butter and sugar until combined. Add the egg gradually; beating well. Transfer to a large mixing bowl and fold in the mashed banana.

2 Sift the flour, baking powder and salt. Stir the flour mixture and milk alternately into the butter mix. Stir until just combined. Set aside 2/3 cup of mixture. Spoon the remaining mixture into the prepared tin and smooth the surface. Bake 35–40 minutes, or until a skewer comes out clean when inserted in the cake.

3 Combine the almonds, corn syrup, cinnamon and reserved cake mixture. Spoon over the cake. Return the cake to the oven for a further 20–25 minutes, or until a skewer inserted into the centre comes out clean. Allow to cool in the tin. Dust with icing sugar.

Coffee and Almond Slice

Makes 24 pieces

125 g (4¹/₂ oz) unsalted butter

185 g (6¹/₂ oz/³/₄ cup) caster (superfine) sugar

1 teaspoon natural vanilla extract

2 eggs, lightly beaten

1 tablespoon instant coffee powder

185 g (6¹/₂ oz/1¹/₂ cups) plain (all-purpose) flour

185 g (6¹/₂ oz/1 cup) ground almonds

45 g (1¹/₂ oz/¹/₂ cup) desiccated coconut

60 g (2¹/₄ oz/²/₃ cup) flaked almonds, lightly toasted

COFFEE BUTTER ICING

60 g (2¹/₄ oz) unsalted butter

2 teaspoons instant coffee powder

125 g (4¹/₂ oz/1 cup) icing (confectioners') sugar

1. Preheat the oven to 180°C (350°F/Gas 4). Lightly grease a 18 x 28 cm (7 x 11 inch) shallow tin and line with baking paper.

2. Beat the butter, sugar and vanilla with electric beaters until creamy. Gradually add the eggs, beating well after each addition. Dissolve the coffee in 1 tablespoon of hot water and beat into the mixture.

3. Sift the flour and mix with the ground almonds and coconut. Fold into the egg and butter mixture in batches. Stir until smooth.

4. Spread the mixture into the tin and smooth the surface. Bake for 25–30 minutes, or until a skewer inserted into the centre comes out clean. Allow to cool in the tin.

5 To make the icing, beat the butter using electric beaters until creamy. Dissolve the coffee in a little hot water. Sift the icing sugar and add to the butter gradually, with the dissolved coffee. Spread the icing over the slice and sprinkle with the flaked almonds. Cut into pieces to serve.

Chocolate Peppermint Slice

Makes 24 pieces

90 g (3¹/4 oz/³/4 cup) self-raising flour

30 g (1 oz/¹/4 cup) unsweetened cocoa powder

45 g (1¹/2 oz/¹/2 cup) desiccated coconut

60 g (2 oz/¹/4 cup) sugar

140 g (5 oz) unsalted butter, melted

1 egg, lightly beaten

PEPPERMINT FILLING

185 g (6¹/2 oz/1¹/2 cups) icing (confectioners') sugar, sifted

30 g (1 oz) Copha (white vegetable shortening), melted

2 tablespoons milk

¹/2 teaspoon peppermint essence

CHOCOLATE TOPPING

185 g (6¹/2 oz) dark chocolate, chopped

30 g (1 oz) Copha (white vegetable shortening)

1 Preheat the oven to 180°C (350°F/Gas 4). Lightly grease a shallow 18 x 28 cm (7 x 11 inches) tin and line with baking paper, leaving the paper hanging over on the two long sides.

2 Sift the flour and cocoa into a bowl. Stir in the coconut and sugar, then add the butter and egg and mix well. Press the mixture firmly into the tin. Bake for 15 minutes, then press down with the back of a spoon and leave to cool.

3 To make the peppermint filling, sift the icing sugar into a bowl. Stir in the Copha, milk and peppermint essence. Spread over the base and refrigerate for 5–10 minutes, or until firm.

4 To make the chocolate topping, put the chocolate and Copha in a heatproof bowl and set over a saucepan of simmering water. Stir occasionally until melted and combined. Spread evenly over the filling. Refrigerate the slice for 20 minutes, or until the chocolate topping is firm. Carefully lift the slice from the tin, using the paper as handles. Cut into pieces with a warm knife to give clean edges.

Chocolate Hedgehog Slice

Makes 50 pieces

250 g (9 oz) chocolate cream biscuits (cookies), finely crushed

45 g (1^1/$_2$ oz/^{1}/$_2$ cup) desiccated coconut

100 g (3^1/$_2$ oz/1 cup) pecans, roughly chopped

1 tablespoon unsweetened cocoa powder, sifted

100 g (3^1/$_2$ oz) dark chocolate, chopped

80 g (2^3/$_4$ oz) unsalted butter

1 tablespoon golden or maple syrup

1 egg, lightly beaten

ICING

100 g (3^1/$_2$ oz) dark chocolate, chopped

40 g (1^1/$_2$ oz) unsalted butter

1 Lightly grease a shallow 30 x 20 cm (12 x 8 inch) rectangular tin and line the base and sides with baking paper.

2 Combine the crushed biscuits, coconut, pecans and cocoa in a mixing bowl. Make a well in the centre.

3 Combine the chocolate, butter and syrup in heavy-based saucepan. Stir over low heat until the chocolate and butter have melted. Pour the combined chocolate mixture and egg onto the dry ingredients. Using a wooden spoon, stir until well combined. Press the mixture evenly into the prepared tin. Refrigerate for 30 minutes until set.

4 To make the icing, put the chocolate and butter in a heatproof bowl. Set over a saucepan of simmering water. Stir until melted. Cool slightly. Spread the mixture evenly over the slice base. Refrigerate until set. Remove the slice from tin. Cut into small squares to serve.

Caramel Pecan Squares

Makes 16 pieces

250 g (9 oz) plain chocolate biscuits (cookies)

20 g (^{3}/4 oz) powdered drinking chocolate, plus extra for dusting

150 g (5^1/2 oz/1^1/2 cups) pecans

185 g (6^1/2 oz) unsalted butter, melted

CARAMEL TOPPING

90 g (3^1/4 oz/^{1}/2 cup) lightly packed soft brown sugar

60 g (2^1/4 oz) unsalted butter

400 g (14 oz) can sweetened condensed milk

1　Preheat the oven to 180°C (350°F/Gas 4). Lightly grease a 18 x 28 cm (7 x 11 inch) shallow tin and line with baking paper, leaving the paper hanging over on the two long sides.

2　Finely crush the biscuits, drinking chocolate and a third of the pecans in a food processor. Transfer to a bowl and add the melted butter. Mix well and press into the tin. Press the rest of the pecans over the top.

3　To make the caramel topping, stir the brown sugar and butter in a saucepan over low heat until the butter melts and the sugar dissolves. Remove from the heat, stir in the milk, then pour over the biscuit base. Bake for 25–30 minutes, or until the caramel is firm and golden. Cool, then refrigerate for at least 3 hours.

4　Trim off the edges and cut the slice into squares. Dust with drinking chocolate to serve.

Layered Chocolate Sponge Cake

Serves 12-16

125 g (4$^{1}/_{2}$ oz/1 cup) plain (all-purpose) flour

30 g (1 oz/$^{1}/_{4}$ cup) unsweetened cocoa powder

$^{1}/_{4}$ teaspoon salt

6 large eggs, separated

$^{1}/_{2}$ teaspoon cream of tartar

275 g (9$^{3}/_{4}$ oz/1$^{1}/_{4}$ cups) sugar

2 teaspoons natural vanilla extract

VIENNA CREAM

160 g (5$^{3}/_{4}$ oz) unsalted butter

500 g (1 lb 2 oz/4 cups) icing (confectioners') sugar, sifted

60 g (2$^{1}/_{4}$ oz/$^{1}/_{2}$ cup) unsweetened cocoa powder

60 ml (2 fl oz/$^{1}/_{4}$ cup) milk

GLACÉ ICING

1 teaspoon instant coffee powder

250 g (9 oz/2 cups) sifted icing (confectioners') sugar

1 tablespoon unsalted butter, melted

1   Preheat the oven to 180°C (350°F/Gas 4). Lightly grease two 23 cm (9 inch) round cake tins and line with baking paper.

2   Beat the egg whites and cream of tartar in large bowl using electric beaters until soft peaks form. Gradually add the sugar and beat until the sugar has dissolved and the mixture is thick.

3   Beat the egg yolks and vanilla slightly. Add the egg yolks to egg whites, beat 20 seconds. Using a metal spoon, fold in the sifted flour, cocoa and salt quickly.

4   Spread the mixture evenly into the tins. Bake for 20 minutes, or until a skewer inserted into the centre comes out clean. Leave the cakes in the tins for 5 minutes before turning out onto wire racks to cool.

5   To make the vienna cream, beat the butter in a small bowl using electric beaters until light and fluffy. Add the icing sugar, cocoa powder and milk. Beat for 8–10 minutes, or until smooth and fluffy.

6   Spread one cake layer with half the vienna cream. Using a piping bag fitted with a star tip, pipe some of the remaining vienna cream around the edge of this cake layer. Top with the other cake layer.

7   To make the glacé icing, dissolve the coffee in hot water. Combine the icing sugar and melted butter in a small heatproof bowl. Stir in the coffee mixture to make a paste. Set the bowl over a saucepan of simmering water. Stir until the icing is smooth and glossy.

8   Quickly spread the icing over the cake using a flat-bladed knife. Dip the knife into hot water occasionally to give a smooth finish. Dust the icing with extra cocoa powder. Pipe the remaining vienna cream around the top edge. Allow the icing to set before serving.

 This cake can be kept unfilled and without icing in an airtight container for up to 3 days.

Chocolate Mud Cake

serves 6–8

250 g (9 oz) unsalted butter
250 g (9 oz) dark chocolate, chopped
2 tablespoons instant coffee powder
150 g (5^1/2 oz/1^1/4 cups) self-raising flour
150 g (5^1/2 oz/1^1/4 cups) plain (all-purpose) flour
60 g (2^1/4 oz/^{1}/2 cup) unsweetened cocoa powder
^{1}/2 teaspoon bicarbonate of soda (baking soda)
550 g (1 lb 4 oz/2^1/4 cups) caster (superfine) sugar
4 eggs, lightly beaten
2 tablespoons oil
125 ml (4 fl oz/^{1}/2 cup) buttermilk

ICING
150 g (5^1/2 oz) unsalted butter, chopped
150 g (5^1/2 oz) dark chocolate, chopped

1   Preheat the oven to 160°C (315°F/Gas 2–3). Lightly grease a deep
    22 cm (8^1/2 inch) round cake tin. Line with baking paper, making sure
    the paper around the side extends at least 5 cm (2 inches) above the
    top edge.

2   Put the butter, chocolate and coffee in a saucepan with 185 ml
    (6 fl oz/^{3}/4 cup) of hot water and stir over low heat until smooth.
    Remove from the heat.

3   Sift the flours, cocoa and bicarbonate of soda into a large bowl. Stir
    in the sugar and make a well in the centre. Add the combined eggs,
    oil and buttermilk and, using a large metal spoon, slowly stir into the
    dry ingredients. Gradually stir in the butter mixture.

4   Pour the mixture into the tin and bake for 1 hour 45 minutes, or until a skewer inserted into the centre comes out clean (the skewer may be slightly wet). Remove the cake from the oven. If the top looks raw, bake for a further 5–10 minutes, then remove. Leave in the tin until completely cold, then turn out onto a wire rack to cool.

5   To make the icing, combine the butter and chocolate in a saucepan and stir over low heat until the butter and chocolate are melted. Remove and cool slightly. Pour over the cake and allow it to run down the side.

 Refrigerate in an airtight container for up to 3 weeks, or store in a cool dry place for up to 1 week. Freeze for up to 2 months.

Espresso Chocolate Cake with Chocolate Liqueur Sauce

serves 6–8

20 g (^{3}/4 oz/^{1}/4 cup) finely ground espresso coffee

150 g (5^1/2 oz) unsalted butter

140 g (5 oz/^{3}/4 cup) soft dark brown sugar

2 eggs, lightly beaten

35 g (1^1/4 oz/^{1}/3 cup) ground almonds

185 g (6^1/2 oz/1^1/2 cups) self-raising flour

30 g (1 oz/^{1}/4 cup) unsweetened cocoa powder

CHOCOLATE LIQUEUR SAUCE

170 g (6 oz/^{3}/4 cup) caster (superfine) sugar

60 ml (2 fl oz/^{1}/4 cup) chocolate liqueur

1 Combine the coffee and 185 ml (6 fl oz/^{3}/4 cup) of water in a small heatproof bowl. Allow to stand for 10 minutes. Strain, reserving 125 ml (4 fl oz/^{1}/2 cup) of the liquid.

2 Preheat the oven to 180°C (350°F/Gas 4). Lightly grease a deep 20 cm (8 inch) baba tin. Beat the butter and sugar in a bowl using electric beaters until light and creamy. Add the eggs gradually, beating thoroughly after each addition.

3 Transfer the mixture to a large bowl and add the almonds. Using a metal spoon, fold in the sifted flour and cocoa alternately with the strained coffee. Stir until just combined and the mixture is smooth.

4 Spoon the mixture into the tin and smooth the surface. Bake for 30 minutes, or until a skewer inserted into the centre comes out clean. Leave in the tin for 15 minutes before turning onto a wire rack.

5   To make the chocolate liqueur sauce, combine the sugar, 185 ml
    (6 fl oz/3/4 cup) of water and liqueur in a small saucepan. Stir
    constantly over low heat until the mixture boils and the sugar has
    dissolved. Reduce the heat, simmer without stirring, uncovered, until
    the mixture begins to thicken and the liquid is reduced by half.
    Remove from the heat. Pour the sauce into a heatproof serving jug.
    Serve the sauce with the cake.

Caramel, Coconut and Walnut Cake

serves 6–8

55 g (2 oz/¹/4 cup) soft brown sugar
20 g (³/4 oz/¹/3 cup) flaked coconut
60 g (2¹/4 oz/¹/2 cup) chopped walnuts
40 g (1¹/2 oz) unsalted butter, melted
2 tablespoons golden or maple syrup
1 madeira (pound) packet cake mix

1 Preheat the oven to 180°C (350°F/Gas 4). Lightly grease a deep, 20 cm (8 inch) round cake tin and line with baking paper.

2 Combine the sugar, coconut, walnuts, butter and syrup in a small bowl and mix well. With slightly damp fingers, spread the mixture evenly over the base of the prepared tin.

3 Make the packet cake mix according to the manufacturer's instructions. Spoon on top of the coconut mixture in the tin. Smooth the surface with a spatula and bake for 35–40 minutes, or until a skewer inserted into the centre comes out clean. Set aside for 5 minutes before turning onto a wire rack to cool.

Use pecans or macadamia nuts in place of the walnuts if you prefer.

Chocolate Brownies

Makes 24 pieces

40 g (1 1/2 oz/1/3 cup) plain (all-purpose) flour

60 g (2 1/4 oz/1/2 cup) unsweetened cocoa powder

500 g (1 lb 2 oz/2 cups) sugar

125 g (4 1/2 oz/1 cup) chopped pecans or walnuts

250 g (9 oz) dark chocolate, chopped into small pieces

250 g (9 oz) unsalted butter, melted

2 teaspoons natural vanilla extract

4 eggs, lightly beaten

1   Preheat the oven to 180°C (350°F/Gas 4). Lightly grease a
    20 x 30 cm (8 x 12 inch) cake tin and line with baking paper,
    leaving the paper hanging over on the two long sides.

2   Sift the flour and cocoa into a bowl and add the sugar, nuts and
    chocolate. Mix together and make a well in the centre.

3   Pour the butter into the dry ingredients with the vanilla and eggs
    and mix well. Pour into the tin, smooth the surface and bake for
    50 minutes (the mixture will still be a bit soft on the inside). Chill for
    at least 2 hours before lifting out, using the paper as handles, and
    cutting into pieces.

Cappuccino Slice

Makes 16 pieces

40 g (1¹/₂ oz/¹/₃ cup) self-raising flour

30 g (1 oz/¹/₄ cup) plain (all-purpose) flour

1 tablespoon unsweetened cocoa powder

60 g (2¹/₄ oz/¹/₄ cup) caster (superfine) sugar

1 egg, lightly beaten

1 teaspoon natural vanilla extract

65 g (2¹/₄ oz) unsalted butter, melted

60 ml (2 fl oz/¹/₄ cup) milk

50 g (1³/₄ oz) dark chocolate, grated

CAPPUCCINO FILLING

350 g (12 oz) cream cheese

100 g (3¹/₂ oz) mascarpone cheese

90 g (3¹/₄ oz/¹/₃ cup) sour cream

90 g (3¹/₄ oz/¹/₃ cup) caster (superfine) sugar

3 eggs, lightly beaten

1 tablespoon instant coffee powder

1   Preheat the oven to 180°C (350°F/Gas 4). Lightly grease a 20 cm (8 inch) square cake tin with baking paper, leaving the paper hanging over on the two long sides.

2   Sift the flours and cocoa into a bowl, stir in the sugar and make a well in the centre. Combine the egg, vanilla, butter and milk and stir into the well until just combined. Spoon into the tin and bake for 10–15 minutes. Allow to cool completely. Reduce the oven to 160°C (315°F/Gas 2–3).

3   To make the filling, beat the cream cheese, mascarpone and sour cream with electric beaters for 3 minutes, or until smooth. Add the sugar in batches and beat for a further 3 minutes. Add the eggs gradually, beating well after each addition.

4   Dissolve the coffee in a little warm water, beat into the filling and pour over the base. Bake for 30–35 minutes, or until set. Leave in the tin to cool completely. Decorate with grated chocolate to serve.

Coffee Syrup Cakes

Makes 6

1¹/2 tablespoons instant coffee powder
90 g (3¹/4 oz/¹/3 cup) sour cream
125 g (4¹/2 oz) unsalted butter
165 g (5³/4 oz/³/4 cup) soft brown sugar
2 eggs
155 g (5¹/2 oz/1¹/4 cups) self-raising flour, sifted

COFFEE SYRUP
2 teaspoons instant coffee powder
165 g (5³/4 oz/³/4 cup) soft brown sugar

1　Preheat the oven to 180°C (350°F/Gas 4). Lightly grease six mini 250 ml (9 fl oz/1 cup) rectangular tins, then lightly dust with flour.

2　Dissolve the coffee in 2 tablespoons of boiling water in a bowl. Allow to cool, then add the sour cream and stir to combine well.

3　Cream the butter and sugar in a bowl using electric beaters until pale and fluffy. Add the eggs one at a time, beating well after each addition. Fold in the flour alternately with the sour cream mixture, then divide the mixture between the prepared tins and smooth the tops. Bake for about 25 minutes, or until a skewer inserted into the centre of a cake comes out clean.

4　To make the coffee syrup, combine the coffee, sugar and 170 ml (5¹/2 fl oz/²/3 cup) water in a small saucepan and stir over medium heat until the sugar has dissolved. Bring to the boil, then remove from the heat. Spoon the hot coffee syrup over the hot cakes in the tins and allow to cool before turning out onto a wire rack.

Coffee Pecan Streusel Muffins

Makes 9

215 g (7^{1}/$_{2}$ oz/1^{3}/$_{4}$ cups) self-raising flour
1 teaspoon baking powder
55 g (2 oz/^{1}/$_{4}$ cup) caster (superfine) sugar
60 g (2^{1}/$_{4}$ oz/^{1}/$_{2}$ cup) finely chopped pecans
1 tablespoon instant coffee powder
1 egg
185 ml (6 fl oz/^{3}/$_{4}$ cup) milk
80 ml (2^{1}/$_{2}$ fl oz/^{1}/$_{3}$ cup) oil

STREUSEL TOPPING
30 g (1 oz) unsalted butter
30 g (1 oz/^{1}/$_{4}$ cup) self-raising flour
2 tablespoons soft brown sugar
1 teaspoon ground cinnamon
2 tablespoons chopped pecans

1   Preheat the oven to 210°C (415°F/Gas 6–7). Lightly grease 9 holes of a 12-hole standard muffin tin. Sift the flour and baking powder into a bowl. Add the caster sugar and pecans. Make a well in the centre.

2   Combine the coffee powder with 1 tablespoon of boiling water. Add to flour mixture with the egg, milk and oil. Stir until just combined.

3   Meanwhile, to make the topping, rub the butter into the flour. Add the sugar, cinnamon and pecans and mix until combined.

4   Divide the mixture among the muffin holes. Sprinkle with the streusel topping and bake for 10–12 minutes, or until golden brown. Transfer to a wire rack to cool.

Chocolate Mousse Torte

Serves 8–10

40 g (1¹/₂ oz/¹/₃ cup) plain (all-purpose) flour

2 tablespoons unsweetened cocoa powder

2 eggs

80 g (2³/₄ oz/¹/₃ cup) caster (superfine) sugar

50 g (1³/₄ oz) dark chocolate, chopped

50 g (1³/₄ oz) unsalted butter, melted

MOUSSE

150 g (5¹/₂ oz) dark chocolate

2 tablespoons caster (superfine) sugar

2 egg yolks

1 teaspoon melted unsalted butter

185 ml (6 fl oz/³/₄ cup) cream (whipping), whipped

2 teaspoons crème de cacao

¹/₂ teaspoon powdered gelatine

60 g (2¹/₄ oz) white chocolate, chopped, to decorate

60 g (2¹/₄ oz) dark chocolate, chopped, to decorate

1   Preheat the oven to 180°C (350°F/Gas 4). Lightly grease a 23 cm (9 inch) recess flan tin. Coat the base and sides evenly with flour and shake off any excess.

2   Beat the eggs in a bowl using electric beaters until thick and pale. Add the sugar gradually, beating constantly until the mixture is pale yellow and glossy and the sugar is dissolved. Transfer the mixture to a large mixing bowl.

3 Put the chocolate in a heatproof bowl and set over a saucepan of simmering water. Stir until melted. Using a metal spoon, fold the melted chocolate, butter, sifted flour and cocoa into the egg mixture quickly and lightly.

4 Spread the mixture evenly in the prepared tin. Bake for 20 minutes, or until the sponge shrinks away from the side of the tin. Stand the sponge in the tin for 5 minutes before turning onto a wire rack to cool.

5 To make the mousse, combine the chocolate, sugar and 60 ml (2 fl oz/$\frac{1}{4}$ cup) of water in a small saucepan. Stir over low heat until the chocolate has melted and the sugar has dissolved; remove the pan from the heat. Transfer the mixture to a large mixing bowl. Whisk in the egg yolks and butter. Beat the mixture until thick and doubled in quantity. Fold in the cream and crème de cacao. Dissolve the gelatine in hot water. Whisk into the chocolate mixture.

6 Spread the chocolate mousse evenly onto the sponge base. Refrigerate until set. Melt the white and dark chocolate separately as for step 3 and drizzle over the top of the cake.

Chocolate Cheesecake Slice

Makes 20 squares

200 g (7 oz) plain chocolate biscuit (cookie) crumbs
80 g (2³/4 oz) unsalted butter, melted
100 g (3¹/2 oz/²/3 cup) chocolate chips

FILLING
375 g (13 oz) cream cheese
110 g (3³/4 oz/¹/2 cup) sugar
3 eggs
150 g (5¹/2 oz) white chocolate, melted

TOPPING
150 g (5¹/2 oz) dark chocolate, melted
160 g (5³/4 oz/²/3 cup) sour cream

1 Preheat the oven to 180°C (350°F/Gas 4). Lightly grease a 20 x 30 cm (8 x 12 inch) rectangular shallow tin. Line with baking paper, leaving the paper hanging over the two long sides.

2 Combine the biscuit crumbs and butter in bowl. Press the mixture into the base of the prepared tin. Sprinkle with chocolate chips.

3 To make the filling, beat the cream cheese in a bowl using electric beaters until creamy. Beat in the sugar. Add the eggs gradually, beating after each addition. Add the chocolate and beat until smooth. Spread the mixture over the base. Bake 30 minutes, or until just set. Cool, cover and refrigerate until firm.

4 To make the topping, put the chocolate and sour cream in a heatproof bowl and set over a saucepan of simmering water. Stir until smooth. Spread over the cheesecake. Refrigerate until firm.

Coffee Hazelnut Muffins

Makes 12

250 g (9 oz/2 cups) self-raising flour

140 g (5 oz/3/4 cup) soft brown sugar

140 g (5 oz/11/4 cups) ground hazelnuts

30 g (1 oz/1/4 cup) chopped roasted hazelnuts

20 g (3/4 oz/1/4 cup) instant coffee powder

310 ml (103/4 fl oz/11/4 cups) buttermilk

2 eggs

125 g (41/2 oz) unsalted butter, melted and cooled

1 Preheat the oven to 180°C (350°F/Gas 4). Lightly grease a 12-hole standard muffin tin and line with paper cases. Sift the flour into a large bowl and add the sugar and nuts. Make a well in the centre.

2 Stir the coffee into the buttermilk until dissolved. Whisk in the eggs and butter. Pour into the well. Fold until just combined — the batter should be lumpy.

3 Divide among the muffin holes. Bake for 20 minutes, or until a skewer inserted into the centre of a muffin comes out clean. Cool in the tin for 5 minutes, then transfer to a wire rack to cool completely.

Caramel Cheesecake

Serves 8–10

BASE

250 g (9 oz) butternut biscuits (cookies), finely crushed

1 tablespoon mixed spice

100 g ($3^1/_2$ oz) unsalted butter, melted

FILLING

500 g (1 lb 2 oz) cream cheese

145 g (5 oz/$^2/_3$ cup) caster (superfine) sugar

1 teaspoon natural vanilla extract

1 tablespoon lemon juice

4 eggs

CARAMEL TOPPING

60 g ($2^1/_4$ oz) unsalted butter

45 g ($1^1/_2$ oz/$^1/_4$ cup) soft or dark brown sugar

125 ml (4 fl oz/$^1/_2$ cup) condensed milk

125 ml (4 fl oz/$^1/_2$ cup) cream (whipping)

1   Lightly grease a 20 cm (8 inch) round spring-form cake tin and line the base with baking paper. Add the crushed biscuits to a bowl and stir in the mixed spice and butter until combined. Spoon into the tin, pressing firmly over the base and side. Refrigerate for 20 minutes.

2   Preheat the oven to 180°C (350°F/Gas 4). To make the filling, beat the cream cheese using electric beaters until smooth. Add the caster sugar, vanilla extract and lemon juice and beat until smooth. Add the eggs, one at a time, beating after each addition. Pour over the crust. Bake for 45–50 minutes, or until just firm.

3   To make the topping, put the butter, brown sugar, condensed milk and cream in a saucepan and stir over low heat until the butter has melted and the sugar dissolved. Bring to the boil and reduce the heat. Simmer gently for 5–10 minutes, stirring continuously to prevent the caramel catching on the bottom of the pan. Remove from the heat and allow to cool. Carefully spread over the cheesecake while still in the tin. Refrigerate in the tin for about 1 hour, or until just set.

Chocolate Hazelnut Friands

Makes 12

200 g (7 oz/1^1/2 cups) hazelnuts
185 g (6^1/2 oz) unsalted butter
6 egg whites
155 g (5^1/2 oz/1^1/4 cups) plain (all-purpose) flour
30 g (1 oz/^{1}/4 cup) unsweetened cocoa powder
250 g (9 oz/2 cups) icing (confectioners') sugar, plus extra for dusting

1 Preheat the oven to 200°C (400°F/Gas 6). Lightly grease twelve
125 ml (4 fl oz/^{1}/2 cup) friand or muffin holes. Spread the hazelnuts
out on a baking tray and bake for 8–10 minutes, or until fragrant. Put
in a clean tea towel (dish towel) and rub vigorously to loosen the
skins. Discard the skins. Cool, then process in a food processor until
finely ground.

2 Put the butter in a small saucepan and melt over medium heat, then
heat for 3–4 minutes, or until it turns a deep golden colour. Strain
any dark solids and set aside to cool.

3 Lightly whisk the egg whites in a bowl until frothy but not firm. Sift
the flour, cocoa powder and icing sugar into a large bowl and stir in
the ground hazelnuts. Make a well in the centre, add the egg whites
and butter and mix until combined.

4 Spoon the mixture into the friand holes until three-quarters filled.
Bake for 20–25 minutes, or until a skewer inserted into the centre
comes out clean. Leave in the tin for a few minutes, then cool on a
wire rack. Dust with icing sugar, to serve.

Chocolate, Ginger and Fig Cake

Serves 8

125 g (4^{1}/$_{2}$ oz) unsalted butter, softened

230 g (8^{1}/$_{2}$ oz/1 cup) soft brown sugar

2 eggs, lightly beaten

185 g (6^{1}/$_{2}$ oz/1^{1}/$_{2}$ cups) self-raising flour

40 g (1^{1}/$_{2}$ oz/^{1}/$_{3}$ cup) unsweetened cocoa powder

185 ml (6 fl oz/^{3}/$_{4}$ cup) milk

125 g (4^{1}/$_{2}$ oz/^{2}/$_{3}$ cup) chopped dried figs

75 g (2^{1}/$_{2}$ oz/^{1}/$_{3}$ cup) chopped glacé ginger

1 Preheat the oven to 180°C (350°F/Gas 4). Lightly grease a
22 x 12 cm (8^{1}/$_{2}$ x 4^{1}/$_{2}$ inch) loaf tin and line the base with
baking paper. Beat the butter and sugar using electric beaters
until creamy.

2 Gradually add the egg, beating well after each addition. Stir in the
sifted flour and cocoa alternately with the milk to make a smooth
batter. Fold in the figs and half the ginger.

3 Spoon the mixture into the prepared tin and smooth the surface.
Scatter the remaining ginger over the top. Bake for 1 hour, or until a
skewer inserted into the centre comes out clean. Leave the cake to
cool in the tin for 5 minutes before turning onto a wire rack to
cool completely.

Black Forest Gâteau

Serves 8–10

125 g (4¹/₂ oz) unsalted butter

250 g (9 oz/1 cup) caster (superfine) sugar

2 eggs, lightly beaten

1 teaspoon natural vanilla extract

40 g (1¹/₂ oz /¹/₃ cup) self-raising flour

125 g (4¹/₂ oz/1 cup) plain (all-purpose) flour

1 teaspoon bicarbonate of soda (baking soda)

60 g (2¹/₄ oz/¹/₂ cup) unsweetened cocoa powder

185 ml (6 fl oz/³/₄ cup) buttermilk

FILLING

60 ml (2 fl oz/¹/₄ cup) Kirsch

750 ml (26 fl oz/3 cups) cream (whipping), lightly whipped

425 g (15 oz) can pitted morello or black cherries, drained

TOPPING

100 g (3¹/₂ oz) dark chocolate

100 g (3¹/₂ oz) milk chocolate

cherries with stalks, to decorate

1 Preheat the oven to 180°C (350°F/Gas 4). Lightly grease a deep, 20 cm (8 inch) round cake tin and line the base and side with baking paper.

2 Beat the butter and sugar using electric beaters until light and creamy. Add the eggs gradually, beating well after each addition. Add the vanilla extract and beat until well combined. Transfer to a large bowl. Using a metal spoon, fold in the sifted flours, bicarbonate of soda and cocoa alternately with the buttermilk. Mix until smooth.

3　Pour the mixture into the tin and smooth the surface. Bake for 50–60 minutes, or until a skewer inserted into the centre comes out clean. Leave the cake in the tin for 30 minutes before turning it onto a wire rack to cool. When cold, cut horizontally into 3 layers, using a long serrated knife. The easiest way to do this is to rest the palm of one hand lightly on top of the cake while cutting into it. Turn the cake every few strokes so the knife cuts in evenly all the way around the edge. When you have gone the whole way round, cut through the middle. Remove the first layer so it will be easier to see what you are doing while cutting the next one.

4　To make the chocolate shavings, leave the chocolate in a warm place for 10–15 minutes, or until soft but still firm. With a vegetable peeler, and using long strokes, shave curls of chocolate from the side of the block. If the block is too soft, chill it to firm it up.

5　To assemble, put one cake layer on a serving plate and brush liberally with Kirsch. Spread evenly with one-fifth of the whipped cream. Top with half the cherries. Continue layering with the remaining cake, liqueur, cream and cherries, finishing with the cream on top. Spread the cream evenly on the outside of the cake. Coat the side with chocolate shavings by laying the shavings on a small piece of baking paper and then pressing them into the cream. Pipe rosettes of cream around the top edge of the cake and decorate with fresh or maraschino cherries on stalks and chocolate shavings.

Coffee Pecan Slice

Makes 15 squares

185 g (6¹/₂ oz/1¹/₂ cups) plain (all-purpose) flour
60 g (2¹/₄ oz/¹/₂ cup) icing (confectioners') sugar
150 g (5¹/₂ oz) unsalted butter

TOPPING
2 tablespoons dark corn syrup
2 tablespoons cream (whipping)
60 g (2¹/₄ oz/¹/₃ cup) soft brown sugar
75 g (2¹/₂ oz) unsalted butter, melted
2 eggs, lightly beaten
1 tablespoon instant coffee powder
200 g (7 oz/2 cups) pecans

1 Preheat the oven to 180°C (350°F/Gas 4). Lightly grease an 18 x 27 cm (7 x 10³/₄ inch) shallow rectangular tin and line with baking paper, leaving the paper hanging over on the two long sides.

2 Put the flour, icing sugar and butter in a food processor bowl and process for 1 minute, or until the mixture comes together. Turn out onto a lightly floured surface and knead the dough for 30 seconds or until smooth. Press into the prepared tin and bake for 15 minutes, or until it is just golden. Cool in the tin.

3 To make the topping, combine the syrup, cream, sugar, butter, eggs and coffee in a bowl and beat with a wooden spoon until smooth. Add the pecans and stir to combine.

4 Pour the topping onto the pastry base. Bake for a further 25 minutes, or until set. Cool in the tin. Lift out and cut into squares.

White Chocolate and Macadamia Nut Brownies

Makes 20 squares

200 g (7 oz) dark chocolate, chopped

100 g (3¹/2 oz) unsalted butter

115 g (4 oz/¹/2 cup) caster (superfine) sugar

2 teaspoons natural vanilla extract

2 eggs, lightly beaten

40 g (1¹/2 oz/¹/3 cup) plain (all-purpose) flour

150 g (5¹/2 oz) white chocolate

110 g (3³/4 oz/²/3 cup) macadamia nuts, chopped

1　Preheat the oven to 180°C (350°F/Gas 4). Lightly grease a 20 cm (8 inch) square cake tin and line with baking paper.

2　Combine the chocolate, 2 tablespoons of water and the butter in a saucepan. Stir over low heat until the chocolate and butter have melted and the mixture is smooth. Stir in the sugar. Remove from the heat.

3　Stir in the vanilla extract, eggs and flour. Mix until well combined.

4　Chop the white chocolate into large chunks. Stir the chocolate and nuts into the mixture. (Stop stirring as soon as chocolate begins to melt.) Spoon the mixture into the prepared tin. Bake for 35 minutes, or until the top is firm to touch. Cool in the tin, then cut into squares.

 Store in an airtight container for up to 3 days.

Mocha Lamingtons

Makes 25

125 g (4 1/2 oz) unsalted butter, chopped, softened
230 g (8 oz/1 cup) caster (superfine) sugar
1/2 teaspoon natural vanilla extract
2 eggs
250 g (9 oz/2 cups) self-raising flour
250 ml (9 fl oz/1 cup) milk
2 teaspoons instant coffee powder

ICING
375 g (13 oz/3 cups) icing (confectioners') sugar
60 g (2 1/4 oz/1/2 cup) unsweetened cocoa powder
20 g (3/4 oz) unsalted butter
2 teaspoons instant coffee powder
75 g (2 1/2 oz/1 1/4 cups) shredded coconut
90 g (3 1/4 oz/1 cup) desiccated coconut

1   Preheat the oven to 180°C (350°F/Gas 4). Lightly grease the base
    of a 23 cm (9 inch) square shallow tin and line the base with
    baking paper.

2   Cream the butter, sugar and vanilla in a bowl using electric beaters
    until pale and fluffy. Add the eggs one at a time, beating well after
    each addition. Sift the flour into a bowl, then stir the flour into the
    butter mixture alternately with the milk until combined and smooth.
    Spoon half the mixture into the prepared tin and spread evenly over
    the base. Dissolve the coffee in 2 teaspoons of boiling water. Add the
    dissolved coffee to the remaining mixture and stir until combined.
    Carefully spread the coffee mixture over the mixture in the tin.

3 Bake for 30–35 minutes, or until a skewer inserted into the centre of the cake comes out clean. Cool in the tin for 5 minutes before turning out onto a wire rack to cool. Cut into 25 squares.

4 To make the icing, sift the icing sugar and cocoa powder into a large shallow bowl. Add the butter and coffee and gradually whisk in 150 ml (5 fl oz) boiling water until smooth. Put the shredded and desiccated coconuts in a large shallow bowl and toss to combine.

5 Using two spoons to hold the cake, dip the cake squares into the icing to cover, allowing the excess to drip off. (Add a little boiling water to the icing if it starts to thicken). Roll the cake in the coconut to cover and place on a wire rack. Repeat with the remaining cakes.

White Chocolate and Hazelnut Slice

Makes 16 pieces

210 g (7½ oz/1½ cups) whole hazelnuts

125 g (4½ oz/1 cup) plain (all-purpose) flour

55 g (2 oz/½ cup) ground hazelnuts

90 g (3¼ oz) white chocolate, chopped

125 g (4½ oz/½ cup) caster (superfine) sugar

100 g (3½ oz) unsalted butter

1 egg

CARAMEL TOPPING

400 g (14 oz) tin condensed milk

2 tablespoons golden or maple syrup

50 g (1¾ oz) unsalted butter

1   Preheat the oven to 180°C (350°F/Gas 4). Lightly grease an 18 x 28 cm (7 x 11 inch) shallow tin with baking paper, leaving the paper hanging over on the two long sides.

2   Put the hazelnuts on a baking tray and bake for 5–8 minutes. Wrap in a tea towel (dish towel) and rub to remove the skins.

3   Sift the flour into a large bowl. Add the ground hazelnuts and make a well in the centre.

4   Put the chocolate, sugar and butter in a saucepan and stir until melted. Cool slightly and pour onto the dry ingredients. Add the egg and mix. Press into the tin. Bake for 20 minutes, then leave to cool.

5   To make the topping, put the condensed milk, syrup and butter in a saucepan. Stir over low heat. Pour over the base, top with the hazelnuts and bake for 15 minutes. Cool before lifting out of the tin.

Choc-Chip and Pistachio Friands

Makes 10

150 g (5¹/2 oz/1 cup) shelled pistachio nuts
60 g (2¹/4 oz/¹/2 cup) plain (all-purpose) flour
175 g (6 oz) unsalted butter
210 g (7¹/2 oz/1²/3 cups) icing (confectioners') sugar
2 tablespoons unsweetened cocoa powder
¹/2 teaspoon ground cardamom
5 egg whites, lightly whisked
200 g (7 oz) chocolate chips
icing (confectioners') sugar, for dusting

1 Preheat the oven to 200°C (400°F/Gas 6). Grease and line ten friand tins, or ten 125 ml (4 fl oz/¹/2 cup) capacity muffin holes. Put the pistachios on a baking tray and roast for 5 minutes. Remove from the oven and allow to cool. Put the pistachios and flour in a food processor and process until finely ground.

2 Put the butter and icing sugar in a bowl and beat until light and creamy. Sift together the pistachios and flour with the cocoa and cardamom, and fold into the creamed mixture.

3 Stir the egg whites into the creamed mixture, together with the chocolate chips, and mix to combine. Spoon the mixture into the prepared tins and bake for 25–30 minutes, or until they come away from the sides of the tin. Cool on wire racks. Dust lightly with icing sugar.

Ganache Torte

serves 8–10

115 g (4 oz) plain sweet biscuits (cookies), crushed
100 g (3¹/₂ oz/1 cup) pecans, crushed
1 tablespoon brown sugar
1 tablespoon desiccated coconut
¹/₄ teaspoon ground cinnamon
90 g (3¹/₄ oz) unsalted butter, melted

FILLING
250 g (9 oz) dark chocolate
80 ml (2¹/₂ fl oz/¹/₃ cup) cream (whipping)
1 teaspoon instant coffee powder
250 ml (9 fl oz/1 cup) cream (whipping), whipped

SAUCE
60 g (2¹/₄ oz) unsalted butter
95 g (3¹/₄ oz/¹/₂ cup) brown sugar
80 ml (2¹/₂ fl oz/¹/₃ cup) cream (whipping)

1 Preheat the oven to 160°C (315°F/Gas 2–3). Lightly grease a 23 cm (9 inch) shallow flan tin (with a removable base).

2 Combine the dry ingredients in a large bowl and add the melted butter. Stir with a wooden spoon until well combined. Press the mixture evenly over the base and sides of the prepared tin. Bake for 20 minutes, then set aside to cool.

3 To make the filling, break the chocolate into small pieces and put in a mixing bowl. Put the cream in a small heavy-based saucepan and

bring to the boil. Pour the hot cream over the chocolate. Using a wooden spoon, stir until the chocolate has melted and the mixture is smooth. Add the coffee powder and stir until dissolved. Pour chocolate mixture into the prepared crust. Refrigerate until set. Remove from the refrigerator 30 minutes before serving.

4   To make the sauce, combine the butter and sugar in a small saucepan. Stir over low heat until the butter has melted and the sugar has dissolved. Remove from the heat. Add the cream and stir with a wooden spoon until well combined. Allow to cool. Serve the torte in thin wedges with sauce and whipped cream.

Flourless Chocolate Cake

Serves 6-8

250 g (9 oz) dark chocolate, chopped
100 g (3¹/2 oz/¹/2 cup) caster (superfine) sugar
100 g (3¹/2 oz) unsalted butter, cubed
1 tablespoon coffee-flavoured liqueur
125 g (4¹/2 oz/1 cup) ground hazelnuts
5 eggs, separated
icing (confectioners') sugar, for dusting

1 Preheat the oven to 180°C (350°F/Gas 4). Lightly grease a 23 cm (9 inch) spring-form cake tin and line the base with baking paper.

2 Put the cooking chocolate, sugar, butter and liqueur in a heatproof bowl and set over a saucepan of simmering water. Stir occasionally until melted. Remove from the heat and mix thoroughly.

3 Transfer the chocolate mixture to a large bowl. Stir in the hazelnuts, then beat in the egg yolks one at a time, mixing well after each addition. In a dry bowl, whisk the egg whites until they form medium stiff peaks. Stir a tablespoonful of the whisked whites into the chocolate, then gently fold in the rest using a large metal spoon or rubber spatula.

4 Pour the mixture into the tin and bake for 50–60 minutes, or until a skewer inserted into the centre comes out clean. Leave to cool completely in the tin, before turning out and dusting with icing sugar.

Crème Caramel Slice

Makes 12 pieces

150 g (5$^{1}/_{2}$ oz) unsalted butter

185 g (6$^{1}/_{2}$ oz/1 cup) soft brown sugar

4 eggs, separated

2 tablespoons golden or maple syrup

30 g (1 oz/$^{1}/_{4}$ cup) plain (all-purpose) flour

250 ml (9 fl oz/1 cup) milk

thickened (whipping) cream and sliced strawberries, to decorate

1 Preheat the oven to 180°C (350°F/Gas 4). Lightly grease an 18 x 28 cm (7 x 11 inch) shallow tin with baking paper, leaving the paper hanging over on the two long sides.

2 Beat the butter and sugar with electric beaters until light and creamy. Add the egg yolks and syrup and beat until well combined. Fold in the flour, alternating with the milk.

3 Beat the egg whites into stiff peaks. Fold into the butter mixture, then pour into the tin.

4 Put the tin in a large baking dish, then pour enough hot water into the dish to reach halfway up the side of the tin. Bake for 30–35 minutes, or until springy and dark golden on top.

5 Remove the tin from the baking dish and leave the slice to cool in the tin before lifting out to cut. Decorate each piece with a dollop of cream and strawberry slices to serve.

Coffee Liqueur Gâteau

Serves 8–10

125 g (4½ oz/¾ cup) brazil nuts
100 g (3½ oz/⅔ cup) blanched almonds
80 g (2¾ oz/½ cup) hazelnuts
2 tablespoons plain (all-purpose) flour
170 g (6 oz/¾ cup) caster (superfine) sugar
7 egg whites
60 ml (2 fl oz/¼ cup) Tia Maria or Kahlua
sifted icing (confectioners') sugar, for dusting

COFFEE CREAM
200 g (7 oz) unsalted butter
150 g (5½ oz) dark chocolate, melted
2–3 teaspoons icing (confectioners') sugar
3–4 teaspoons instant coffee powder

1 Preheat the oven to 180°C (350°F/Gas 4). Lightly grease a deep 20 cm (8 inch) round tin. Line the base and sides with baking paper.

2 Put the nuts on a baking tray. Roast for 5–10 minutes, or until golden. Rub the nuts vigorously in a clean tea towel (dish towel) to remove the hazelnut skins. Put nuts in a food processor and process until finely ground.

3 Transfer the nuts to a large bowl. Add the flour and 115 g (4 oz/ ½ cup) of the sugar and mix well. Beat the egg whites in large bowl using electric beaters until soft peaks form. Gradually add the remaining sugar, beating until mixture is thick and glossy and the sugar is dissolved. Using a metal spoon, fold the nut mixture into

the egg mixture a third at a time. Spoon into the prepared tin and smooth the surface. Bake for 35–40 minutes, or until springy to the touch. Leave the cake in the tin to cool completely.

4 To make the coffee cream, beat the butter in a bowl using electric beaters until creamy. Gradually pour in the melted chocolate, beating until well combined. Dissolve the coffee in 2 teaspoons of warm water. Add the icing sugar and coffee mixture and beat until smooth.

5 To assemble the gateau, turn the cake onto a flat working surface. Using a sharp serrated knife, carefully cut the cake horizontally into three layers. (Use the top layer of cake as the base of the gateau.) Brush the first layer with half the liqueur. Spread with one-fifth of the coffee cream.

6 Put the second cake layer on top. Brush with the remaining liqueur and spread with a quarter of the remaining cream. Put the remaining layer on top. Spread the top and sides with the remaining cream.

7 Dust the cake with icing sugar. Refrigerate for 1 hour, or until firm.

Choc-Chip Muffins

Makes 12

310 g (11 oz/2¹/2 cups) self-raising flour
95 g (3¹/4 oz/¹/2 cup) soft brown sugar
375 ml (13 fl oz/1¹/2 cups) milk
2 eggs, lightly beaten
1 teaspoon natural vanilla extract
150 g (5¹/2 oz) unsalted butter, melted and cooled
260 g (9¹/4 oz/1³/4 cups) chocolate chips

1   Preheat the oven to 200°C (400°F/Gas 6). Lightly grease a 12-hole standard muffin tin. Sift the flour into a bowl to aerate the flour and ensure a light muffin. Add the chocolate chips and sugar to the bowl and stir through the flour. Make a well in the centre.

2   In a jug, mix together the milk, eggs and vanilla extract. Pour the liquid into the well in the flour and add the cooled butter.

3   Fold the mixture gently with a metal spoon until just combined. Divide the mixture evenly among the muffin holes using two metal spoons. Fill each hole to about three-quarters full.

4   Bake the muffins for 20–25 minutes, or until golden and a skewer inserted into the centre of a muffin comes out clean. Leave to cool in the tin for 5 minutes. Using a flat-bladed knife, loosen the muffins and transfer to a wire rack to cool completely.

Individual Chocolate Cakes

Makes 12

75 g (2 1/2 oz) unsalted butter

75 g (2 1/2 oz) milk chocolate, chopped

80 g (2 3/4 oz/1/3 cup) brown sugar

2 eggs, lightly beaten

60 g (2 1/4 oz/1/2 cup) self-raising flour, sifted

GANACHE

80 g (2 3/4 oz) milk chocolate, chopped

2 tablespoons thickened (whipping) cream

1 Preheat the oven to 160°C (315°F/Gas 2–3). Line a flat-bottomed 12-hole cupcake tray with paper cases. Put the butter and chocolate in a heatproof bowl and set over a saucepan of simmering water. Stir until melted and combined. Remove the bowl from the heat, add the sugar and egg and mix. Stir in the flour.

2 Transfer the mixture to a measuring jug and pour into the paper cases. Bake for 20–25 minutes, or until cooked. Leave in the tin for 10 minutes, then transfer to a wire rack to cool.

3 To make the ganache, put the chocolate and cream in a heatproof bowl and set over a saucepan of simmering water. Once the chocolate has almost melted, remove the bowl from the heat and stir until the remaining chocolate has melted and the mixture is smooth. Allow to cool for about 8 minutes, or until thickened slightly. Spread one heaped teaspoon of the ganache over the top of each cake.

Devil's Food Cake

Serves 8–10

280 g (10 oz/1¹/2 cups) soft brown sugar

40 g (1¹/2 oz/¹/3 cup) unsweetened cocoa powder

250 ml (9 fl oz/1 cup) milk

90 g (3¹/4 oz) dark chocolate, chopped

125 g (4¹/2 oz) unsalted butter, softened

1 teaspoon natural vanilla extract

2 eggs, separated

185 g (6¹/2 oz/1¹/2 cups) plain (all-purpose) flour

1 teaspoon bicarbonate of soda (baking soda)

CHOCOLATE ICING

50 g (1³/4 oz) dark chocolate, chopped

30 g (1 oz) unsalted butter

1 tablespoon icing (confectioners') sugar

FILLING

250 ml (9 fl oz/1 cup) cream (whipping)

1 tablespoon icing (confectioners') sugar

1 teaspoon natural vanilla extract

1 Preheat the oven to 160°C (315°F/Gas 2–3). Lightly grease two deep 20 cm (8 inch) round cake tins and line the bases with baking paper. Combine a third of the brown sugar with the cocoa and milk in a small saucepan. Stir over low heat until the sugar and cocoa have dissolved. Remove from the heat and stir in the chocolate, stirring until it is melted. Allow to cool.

2   Cream the remaining brown sugar with the butter in a small bowl using electric beaters until light and fluffy. Beat in the vanilla and egg yolks and the cooled chocolate mixture. Transfer to a large bowl, and stir in the sifted flour and bicarbonate of soda.

3   Beat the egg whites in a small bowl until soft peaks form. Fold into the chocolate mixture. Divide the mixture evenly between the tins. Bake for 35 minutes, or until a skewer inserted in the centre of the cakes comes out clean. Leave in the tins for 5 minutes before turning out onto a wire rack to cool.

4   To make the icing, put the chocolate and butter in a heatproof bowl and set over a saucepan of simmering water. Stir until the mixture is melted. Gradually add the sifted icing sugar and stir until smooth.

5   To make the filling, whip the cream, icing sugar and vanilla in a small bowl using electric beaters until stiff peaks form. Spread over one of the cold cakes, top with the second cake and spread the top and sides with icing.

Chocolate Pudding Caramel Cream Tart

puddings, pies and tarts

Caramel Bread Pudding Cappuccino Tarts

Vanilla and Caramel Swirl Ice Cream Pie

serves 6–8

250 g (9 oz) plain chocolate biscuits (cookies)
150 g (5¹/2 oz) unsalted butter, melted
1 vanilla bean, split
250 ml (9 fl oz/1 cup) milk
500 ml (17 fl oz/2 cups) cream (whipping)
160 g (5¹/2 oz/²/3 cup) caster (superfine) sugar
6 egg yolks

CARAMEL
125 g (4¹/2 oz/¹/2 cup) caster (superfine) sugar
60 ml (2 fl oz/¹/4 cup) cream (whipping)
30 g (1 oz) unsalted butter

1   Lightly grease a 27 x 16 x 5 cm (11 x 6¹/4 x 2 inch) deep pie dish. Finely crush the biscuits in a food processor. Stir in the butter and mix until well combined. Spoon into the dish, pressing evenly and firmly over the base and side. Refrigerate.

2   Scrape the seeds from the vanilla bean into a saucepan. Add the pod, milk, cream and sugar and stir over medium heat until the sugar dissolves.

3   Whisk the egg yolks in a small bowl and slowly whisk in about 125 ml (4 fl oz/¹/2 cup) of the warm cream mixture. Return this mixture to the saucepan and cook over low heat, stirring constantly, for 10 minutes, or until the custard thickens and coats the back of a spoon. Strain into a bowl and refrigerate for 20 minutes.

4 Pour the mixture into a shallow baking tray and freeze for 1½ hours, or until frozen around the edges. Transfer to a large bowl or food processor and beat until smooth. Pour back into the tray and return to the freezer. Repeat this three times. For the final freezing, pour the mixture into the pie dish and cover with baking paper.

5 To make the caramel, put the sugar and 1 tablespoon of water in a small saucepan and stir over low heat until the sugar has dissolved, brushing down the side of the pan with a clean pastry brush dipped in water if any crystals appear. Increase the heat, bring to the boil and cook, without stirring, until pale caramel. Remove from the heat and gradually add the cream, butter and 1 tablespoon of water. Return to the heat and bring to the boil, stirring well. Remove and cool for 20 minutes. When slightly warm, spoon the caramel over the pie. Freeze until hard. Serve with any remaining caramel.

Chocolate Pudding

Serves 6

90 g (3^1/$_4$ oz) unsalted butter

95 g (3^1/$_4$ oz/^{1}/$_2$ cup) soft brown sugar

3 eggs, separated

125 g (4^1/$_2$ oz) dark chocolate, melted and cooled

1 teaspoon natural vanilla extract

125 g (4^1/$_2$ oz/1 cup) self-raising flour

1 tablespoon unsweetened cocoa powder

^{1}/$_2$ teaspoon bicarbonate of soda (baking soda)

60 ml (2 fl oz/^{1}/$_4$ cup) milk

2 tablespoons brandy

rich chocolate sauce (see page 206), to serve

1   Preheat the oven to 180°C (350°F/Gas 4). Grease a 1.25 litre (44 fl oz/5 cup) capacity ovenproof dish. Cream the butter and half the sugar until creamy. Beat in the egg yolks, chocolate and vanilla. Fold in the flour, cocoa and bicarbonate of soda, alternating with the milk and brandy. Beat the egg whites until soft peaks form. Beat in the remaining sugar and fold into the chocolate mix.

2   Pour into the dish. Cover with foil and secure with string. Put in a deep ovenproof dish and pour in enough hot water to come halfway up the side of the dish. Bake for 1 hour 25 minutes, or until a skewer inserted into the centre comes out clean. Unmould onto a serving plate.

3   Serve the pudding with cream and rich chocolate sauce.

Sticky Date Pudding with Caramel Sauce

Serves 6–8

370 g (13 oz) pitted dates

1¹/2 teaspoons bicarbonate of soda (baking soda)

1 teaspoon grated fresh ginger

90 g (3¹/4 oz) unsalted butter

250 g (9 oz/1 cup) caster (superfine) sugar

3 eggs

185 g (6¹/2 oz/1¹/2 cups) self-raising flour

¹/2 teaspoon mixed spice

caramel sauce (see page 207), to serve

crème fraîche, to serve

1 Preheat the oven to 180°C (350°/Gas 4). Grease and line the base of a deep 23 cm (9 inch) round cake tin. Chop the dates and put them in a saucepan with 440 ml (15¹/2 fl oz/1³/4 cups) of water. Bring to the boil, then remove from the heat. Add the bicarbonate of soda and ginger and leave to stand for 5 minutes.

2 Cream together the butter, sugar and 1 egg using electric beaters. Beat in the remaining eggs one at a time. Fold in the sifted flour and spice, add the date mixture and stir until well combined. Pour into the tin and bake for 1 hour, or until a skewer inserted into the centre comes out clean. Cover with foil if overbrowning during cooking. Leave to stand for 5 minutes before turning out onto a serving plate.

3 Brush some caramel sauce over the top and sides of the pudding until well-glazed. Serve immediately with the sauce and a dollop of crème fraîche.

Chocolate Tart with Espresso Cones

Serves 8

20 g (³/₄ oz/¹/₄ cup) instant coffee powder

1 litre (35 fl oz/4 cups) vanilla ice cream, softened

TART BASE

100 g (3¹/₂ oz/1 cup) pecans

100 g (3¹/₂ oz) dark chocolate-flavoured biscuits (cookies)

1 tablespoon unsweetened cocoa powder

3 teaspoons soft brown sugar

1 tablespoon dark rum

30 g (1 oz) unsalted butter, melted

40 g (1¹/₂ oz) dark chocolate, melted

FILLING

200 g (7 oz) dark chocolate

30 g (1 oz) unsalted butter

125 ml (4 fl oz/¹/₂ cup) cream (whipping)

3 egg yolks, lightly beaten

250 ml (9 fl oz/1 cup) cream (whipping), whipped

1   To mould the ice cream into shape for the espresso cones, first prepare the moulds. Cover 8 large cream horn moulds with baking paper and secure with sticky tape. Pull the paper off the moulds and transfer the paper cones to the inside of the moulds. Stand the lined cream horn moulds, points down, in mugs to make it easier to spoon in the ice cream.

2   Using a metal spoon, mix the coffee powder with 1 tablespoon of hot water and fold through the ice cream in a bowl. Stir until smooth, then spoon into the paper inside the moulds, before freezing overnight.

3   To make the tart base, lightly grease a shallow, 23 cm (9 inch) round fluted tart tin. Process all the ingredients in short bursts in a food processor for 30 seconds, or until even and crumbly. Press into the base and side of the tin. Refrigerate until firm.

4   To make the filling, stir the chocolate, butter and cream together in a heavy-based saucepan over low heat until melted and smooth. Remove from the heat. Whisk in the egg yolks and transfer to a bowl. Cool slightly. Using a metal spoon, fold in the cream. Stir until smooth. Pour into the tart base, then refrigerate until set. Serve a wedge of the tart with each espresso cone.

Sticky Chocolate Espresso Pudding

serves 8–10

125 g (4¹/₂ oz) unsalted butter
185 g (6¹/₂ oz/1 cup) soft brown sugar
125 g (4¹/₂ oz/¹/₂ cup) caster (superfine) sugar
3 eggs
30 g (1 oz/¹/₂ cup) instant coffee powder
250 g (9 oz/2 cups) plain (all-purpose) flour
60 g (2¹/₄ oz/¹/₂ cup) unsweetened cocoa powder
1 teaspoon bicarbonate of soda (baking soda)
125 g (4¹/₂ oz/¹/₂ cup) sour cream
coffee cream sauce (see page 216), to serve
thick (double/heavy) cream, to serve

1 Preheat the oven to 180°C (350°F/Gas 4). Lightly grease a 25 cm (10 inch) round spring-form cake tin. Line the base with baking paper.

2 Beat the butter and sugars together using electric beaters until light and creamy. Add the eggs one at a time, beating well after each addition. Dissolve the coffee powder in 170 ml (5¹/₂ fl oz/ ²/₃ cup) of hot water. Using a metal spoon, fold the coffee liquid into the butter mixture alternately with the sifted flour, cocoa and bicarbonate of soda. Fold in the sour cream. Mix until just combined.

3 Carefully spoon the mixture into the prepared tin and smooth the surface. Bake for 55 minutes, or until a skewer inserted into the centre of the pudding comes out clean. Cover the pudding with foil for the last 15 minutes of baking if it starts becoming too brown on top.

4 Remove the pudding from the oven and while it is still hot, brush the top with a little of the coffee cream sauce. Allow the pudding to cool slightly before removing it from the tin. Put the pudding on a serving plate and brush it again with the sauce. Serve warm, cut into wedges and drizzled with the remaining coffee cream sauce and thick cream, if desired.

Chocolate Croissant Pudding

Serves 6-8

4 croissants, torn into pieces
125 g (4¹/2 oz) dark chocolate, chopped
4 eggs
100 g (3¹/2 oz) caster (superfine) sugar
250 ml (9 fl oz/1 cup) milk
250 ml (9 fl oz/1 cup) cream (whipping)
3 teaspoons orange liqueur
3 teaspoons grated orange zest
80 ml (2¹/2 fl oz/¹/3 cup) orange juice
40 g (1¹/2 oz) hazelnuts, roughly chopped
cream (whipping), to serve

1 Preheat the oven to 180°C (350°F/Gas 4). Lightly grease a 20 cm (8 inch) deep-sided cake tin and line the base with baking paper. Put the croissant pieces into the tin, then scatter over 100 g (3¹/2 oz) of the dark chocolate.

2 Beat the eggs and sugar together until pale and creamy. Heat the milk, cream and liqueur and remaining chocolate in a saucepan until almost boiling. Stir to melt the chocolate, then remove from the heat. Add to the egg mixture, stirring. Stir in the orange zest and juice. Pour the mixture over the croissants, allowing the liquid to be fully absorbed before adding more.

3 Sprinkle the hazelnuts over the top and bake for 50 minutes, or until a skewer inserted into the centre comes out clean. Cool for 10 minutes. Turn the pudding out and invert onto a serving plate. Slice and serve warm with a dollop of cream.

Chocolate and Peanut Butter Pie

serves 10–12

200 g (7 oz) chocolate biscuits (cookies) with cream centres, crushed
50 g (1 3/4 oz) unsalted butter, melted
200 g (7 oz) cream cheese
85 g (3 oz/2/3 cup) icing (confectioners') sugar, sifted
100 g (3 1/2 oz/2/3 cup) smooth peanut butter
1 teaspoon natural vanilla extract
250 ml (9 fl oz/1 cup) cream (whipping), whipped to firm peaks
60 ml (2 fl oz/1/4 cup) cream (whipping), extra
15 g (1/8 oz) unsalted butter, extra
50 g (1 3/4 oz) dark chocolate, grated
honey-roasted peanuts, chopped, to serve

1 Combine the biscuit crumbs with the melted butter. Press into the base and side of a deep 23 x 18 x 3 cm (9 x 7 x 1 1/4 inch) pie dish. Refrigerate for 15 minutes, or until firm.

2 Beat the cream cheese and icing sugar in a bowl using electric beaters until smooth. Add the peanut butter and vanilla and beat together. Stir in a third of the whipped cream until smooth, then gently fold in the remaining whipped cream. Pour the mixture into the pie shell. Refrigerate for 2 hours, or until firm.

3 Put the extra cream and butter in a saucepan and stir over medium heat until the butter is melted. Remove from the heat, add the grated chocolate, and stir until melted. Cool a little, then dribble the chocolate over the top of the pie to create a lattice pattern. Refrigerate for 2 hours, or until the topping and chocolate are firm. Scatter over the chopped peanuts, to serve.

Caramel Cream Tart

Serves 6–8

125 g (4¹/2 oz) plain sweet biscuits (cookies)
55 g (2 oz/¹/2 cup) ground almonds
90 g (3¹/4 oz) butter or margarine, melted
230 g (8¹/2 oz/1 cup) caster (superfine) sugar
310 ml (10³/4 fl oz/1¹/4 cups) hot milk
3 eggs, separated
3 teaspoons powdered gelatine
170 ml (5¹/2 fl oz/²/3 cup) cream (whipping)
whipped cream and toasted flaked almonds, to serve (optional)

1 Lightly grease a 23 cm (9 inch) flan tin. Crush the biscuits into fine crumbs and put into a bowl. Mix in the ground almonds and then stir in the melted butter. When combined, press over the base and sides of the prepared tin. Refrigerate.

2 Put 115 g (4 oz/¹/2 cup) of the sugar and 80 ml (2¹/2 fl oz/¹/3 cup) of water into a saucepan. Stir over low heat until the sugar has dissolved. Increase the heat and boil rapidly, without stirring, until the mixture is a golden brown colour. Remove from the heat.

3 Slowly stir in the hot milk, return to the heat and stir until the caramel has dissolved in the milk. Beat the egg yolks with the rest of the sugar in a heatproof bowl until thick and creamy.

4 Sprinkle the gelatine into 60 ml (2 fl oz/¹/4 cup) of hot water. Stir until dissolved. Slowly stir the caramel into the egg yolks mixture. Add the dissolved gelatine and stir well. Set the bowl over a saucepan of simmering water. Stir for about 5 minutes. Remove from the heat and put aside until almost set.

5 Beat the egg whites until stiff but not dry. Beat the cream until it begins to thicken. Fold the cream into the custard and then fold in the egg whites. Turn into the base and chill until set. Decorate with cream and top with toasted flaked almonds.

 This tart can be made a day ahead. Store in an airtight container. Decorate with the cream and almonds just before serving.

Chocolate Mousse Flan

Serves 8-10

200 g (7 oz) chocolate biscuits (cookies), finely crushed
100 g (3^1/$_2$ oz) unsalted butter, melted

CHOCOLATE CREAM
100 g (3^1/$_2$ oz) dark chocolate
60 ml (2 fl oz/^{1}/$_4$ cup) thickened (whipping) cream

MOCHA MOUSSE
200 g (7 oz) dark chocolate, melted
60 g (2^1/$_4$ oz) unsalted butter, melted
60 ml (2 fl oz/^{1}/$_4$ cup) thickened (whipping) cream
2 egg yolks
2 teaspoons instant coffee powder
2 teaspoons powdered gelatine
185 ml (6 fl oz/^{3}/$_4$ cup) thickened (whipping) cream, extra

unsweetened cocoa powder, for dusting

1   Lightly grease a 23 cm (9 inch) loose-based fluted flan tin. Combine the biscuit crumbs and butter in a bowl. Press the mixture into the base and sides of the prepared tin. Refrigerate for 20 minutes.

3   To make the chocolate cream, put the chocolate and cream in a small heatproof bowl and set over a saucepan of simmering water. Stir until the chocolate melts and the mixture is smooth. Spread evenly over the base of the prepared flan. Refrigerate until set.

4   To make the mocha mousse, combine the chocolate, butter, cream and yolks in a bowl and mix well. Combine the coffee and 1 teaspoon of boiling water. Add to the mixture.

5   Sprinkle the gelatine over 1 tablespoon of water in a small bowl. Set the bowl over a saucepan of hot water, stirring until the gelatine dissolves. Add the gelatine mixture to the chocolate mixture and stir with a wooden spoon until smooth.

6   Using electric beaters, beat the cream in a large bowl until soft peaks form. Using a metal spoon, fold into the chocolate mixture. Spread over the prepared flan. Refrigerate until set.

7   Dust the flan with cocoa powder. Serve in wedges with cream or ice cream, if desired.

 This flan can be made a day ahead. Store in an airtight container.

Chocolate and Cinnamon Self-Saucing Puddings

Serves 4

50 g (1³/₄ oz/¹/₃ cup) dark chocolate, chopped
60 g (2¹/₄ oz) unsalted butter, cubed
2 tablespoons unsweetened cocoa powder, sifted
160 ml (5¹/₄ fl oz) milk
125 g (4¹/₂ oz/1 cup) self-raising flour
115 g (4 oz/¹/₂ cup) caster (superfine) sugar
80 g (2³/₄ oz/¹/₃ cup) soft brown sugar
1 egg, at room temperature, lightly beaten
thick (double/heavy) cream, to serve

CINNAMON SAUCE
1¹/₂ teaspoons ground cinnamon
50 g (1³/₄ oz) unsalted butter, cubed
60 g (2¹/₄ oz/¹/₃ cup) soft brown sugar
30 g (1 oz/¹/₄ cup) unsweetened cocoa powder, sifted

1 Preheat the oven to 180°C (350°F/Gas 4). Lightly grease four 250 ml (9 fl oz/1 cup) ramekins.

2 Combine the chocolate, butter, cocoa and milk in a saucepan. Stir over low heat until the chocolate has melted. Remove from the heat.

3 Sift the flour into a large bowl and stir in the sugars. Add to the chocolate mixture with the egg and mix well. Spoon the mixture into the prepared dishes, put on a baking tray and set aside.

4 To make the cinnamon sauce, put 375 ml (13 fl oz/1½ cups) of water in a small saucepan. Add the cinnamon, butter, brown sugar and cocoa and stir over low heat until combined. Pour the sauce onto the puddings over the back of a spoon.

5 Bake for 40 minutes, or until firm. Turn out the puddings and serve with thick cream.

Black and White Chocolate Tart

Serves 12

PASTRY

90 g (3^{1}/$_{4}$ oz) unsalted butter, at room temperature

55 g (2 oz/^{1}/$_{4}$ cup) caster (superfine) sugar

1 egg, lightly beaten

185 g (6^{1}/$_{2}$ oz/1^{1}/$_{2}$ cups) plain (all-purpose) flour

30 g (1 oz/^{1}/$_{4}$ cup) self-raising flour

30 g (1 oz/^{1}/$_{4}$ cup) unsweetened cocoa powder

WHITE CHOCOLATE FILLING

2 x 6 g (^{1}/$_{8}$ oz) sheets leaf gelatine

200 ml (7 fl oz) milk

115 g (4 oz/^{1}/$_{2}$ cup) caster (superfine) sugar

80 g (2^{3}/$_{4}$ oz/^{1}/$_{2}$ cup) white chocolate, chopped

4 egg yolks, lightly beaten

250 ml (9 fl oz/1 cup) cream (whipping), lightly whipped

CHOCOLATE GLAZE

60 ml (2 fl oz/^{1}/$_{4}$ cup) cream (whipping)

80 g (2^{3}/$_{4}$ oz/^{1}/$_{2}$ cup) dark chocolate, chopped

10 g (^{1}/$_{4}$ oz) unsalted butter, cubed

2 teaspoons liquid glucose

1   Preheat the oven to 190°C (375°F/Gas 5). Lightly grease a 20 cm (8 inch) spring-form cake tin and line the base with baking paper.

2   To make the pastry, beat the butter using electric beaters until smooth and fluffy. Beat in the sugar and egg until combined. Sift in the combined flours and cocoa powder and stir until the dough

comes together. Knead briefly on a lightly floured surface until smooth. Flatten into a disc, wrap in plastic wrap and refrigerate for 30 minutes.

3 Roll the pastry between two sheets of baking paper until large enough to line the base of the prepared tin. Ease the pastry into the tin and trim any excess pastry so only the base of the tin is covered with pastry. Lightly prick the base of the pastry with a fork. Bake for 15 minutes, or until slightly firm to touch. Set aside to cool.

4 Meanwhile, to make the white chocolate filling, soak the leaf gelatine in 2 tablespoons of cold water for 5 minutes. Heat the milk, sugar and chocolate in a saucepan until simmering. Stir until the sugar has dissolved and the chocolate has melted. Put the egg yolks in a bowl and whisk in the warm milk mixture. Return the mixture to a clean saucepan and stir over medium heat until the mixture lightly coats the back of a spoon. Add the softened gelatine and stir until dissolved. Put the mixture over a bowl of ice and beat until cold. Fold in the cream. Pour the mixture into the pastry case and refrigerate overnight, or until set. Remove the tart from the tin.

5 To make the chocolate glaze, put the cream, chocolate, butter and glucose in a saucepan and stir over low heat until smooth. Allow the glaze to cool slightly until thickened. Spoon the glaze over the top of the tart, allowing it to drip down the side. Use a metal spatula to smooth the glaze over the top of the tart. Set aside at room temperature for 1 hour, or until the glaze is set.

Dark Chocolate Pudding with Mocha Sauce

Serves 6

155 g (5¹/2 oz/1¹/4 cups) self-raising flour
125 g (4¹/2 oz/1 cup) plain (all-purpose) flour
30 g (1 oz/¹/4 cup) unsweetened cocoa powder
¹/4 teaspoon bicarbonate of soda (baking soda)
150 g (5¹/2 oz) unsalted butter
115 g (4 oz/¹/2 cup) caster (superfine) sugar
45 g (1¹/2 oz/¹/4 cup) dark brown sugar
100 g (3¹/2 oz) dark chocolate, chopped
1 teaspoon natural vanilla extract
2 eggs, lightly beaten
185 ml (6 fl oz/³/4 cup) buttermilk
175 g (6 oz/1 cup) dark chocolate chips
mocha sauce (see page 212), to serve

1 Grease a 2 litre (70 fl oz/8 cup) capacity ovenproof dish. Line the base with baking paper. Grease a large sheet of foil and a large sheet of baking paper. Lay the paper over the foil, greased side up. Pleat paper in the centre. Set aside.

2 Sift flours, cocoa and bicarbonate of soda into a large mixing bowl. Make a well in the centre. Combine butter, sugars, chocolate and vanilla in a saucepan. Stir over low heat until the butter and chocolate have melted and the sugars have dissolved. Remove from the heat. Add the butter mixture, beaten eggs and buttermilk to the flour mixture. Using a wooden spoon, stir until well combined. Stir in the chocolate chips.

3   Spoon the mixture into the prepared dish. Cover with the greased foil and paper, greased side down. Put a lid over the foil and secure clips. If you have no lid, lay a pleated tea towel (dish towel) over the foil; tie securely with string under the lip of the basin. Knot the four corners of the tea towel together; use as a handle to help lower the dish into the pan. Put the dish on a trivet in a large, deep pan. Carefully pour boiling water down the side of the pan to come halfway up the side of the basin. Bring to the boil. Cover and cook for 1 hour 15 minutes. Do not let the pudding boil dry; replenish with boiling water as the pudding is cooking. When cooked, invert onto a serving plate. Serve hot with the mocha sauce.

 Store the pudding, covered, in the refrigerator for up to three days until ready to use. The pudding and sauce can be reheated in a microwave or conventional oven.

Crustless Chocolate Tart

Serves 6

500 ml (17 fl oz/2 cups) milk
1/2 cinnamon stick (optional)
1 teaspoon finely chopped lemon zest
1 teaspoon finely chopped orange zest
30 g (1 oz) unsalted butter
60 g (2 1/4 oz/1/2 cup) plain (all-purpose) flour
1 tablespoon unsweetened cocoa powder
3/4 teaspoon baking powder
115 g (4 oz/1/2 cup) caster (superfine) sugar
2 eggs, separated
1/2 teaspoon natural vanilla extract
mocha sauce (see page 212), to serve
thickened (whipping) cream, to serve

1 Preheat the oven to 180°C (350°F/Gas 4). Lightly grease a 23 cm (9 inch) pie dish. Put the milk, cinnamon, zest and butter in a saucepan. Bring to the boil. Remove from the heat. Strain the milk into a bowl, discarding the cinnamon and zest.

2 Combine the sifted flour, cocoa, baking powder and sugar. Combine the milk, egg yolks and essence and beat into the flour mixture. Transfer the mixture to a saucepan. Heat, stirring, until boiling. Reduce the heat and simmer for 3 minutes. Remove from the heat.

3 Beat the egg whites in a clean, dry bowl using electric beaters until stiff peaks form. Using a metal spoon, fold into the cocoa mixture. Pour into the prepared dish. Bake for 30 minutes, or until set. Serve cut in wedges with the mocha sauce and cream.

Caramel Rice Pudding

Serves 4

110 g (3³/4 oz/¹/2 cup) short- or medium-grain rice
2 eggs
2 tablespoons soft brown sugar
375 ml (13 fl oz/1¹/2 cups) milk
2 tablespoons caramel topping
125 ml (4 fl oz/¹/2 cup) cream (whipping)
¹/2 teaspoon freshly grated nutmeg, plus extra, to serve

1 Preheat the oven to 160°C (315°F/Gas 2–3). Grease a 1.5 litre (52 fl oz/6 cups) ovenproof dish. Cook the rice in a saucepan of boiling water for 12 minutes, or until just tender. Drain and then allow the rice to cool slightly.

2 Put the eggs, sugar, milk, caramel topping and cream in a large bowl and whisk together well. Fold in the cooked rice. Pour the rice mixture into the prepared dish and sprinkle the surface with the nutmeg. Put the dish in a deep baking tin and pour in enough boiling water to come halfway up the sides.

3 Bake for 30 minutes, then stir with a fork to distribute the rice evenly. Cook for a further 30 minutes, or until the custard is just set. Serve hot or warm. Sprinkle with the extra ground nutmeg just before serving.

Cappuccino Tarts

Makes 6

185 g (6¹/₂ oz/1¹/₂ cups) plain (all-purpose) flour
60 g (2¹/₄ oz/¹/₄ cup) caster (superfine) sugar
1 teaspoon ground cinnamon
125 g (4¹/₂ oz) unsalted butter, cubed
2 egg yolks

FILLING
500 ml (17 fl oz) vanilla ice cream
1 tablespoon instant coffee powder

TOPPING
2 egg whites
3 tablespoons caster (superfine) sugar
185 ml (6 fl oz/³/₄ cup) cream (whipping)
drinking chocolate or ground cinnamon, for sprinkling

1 Process the flour, sugar, cinnamon and butter in short bursts until fine and crumbly. Add the egg yolks and 1 tablespoon of water and process for a further 15 seconds, or until the mixture comes together. Turn out onto a floured surface and gather the dough together to make a smooth ball. Preheat the oven to 180°C (350°F/Gas 4).

2 Cut the dough into 6 even pieces and roll each out thinly to line six 10 cm (4 inch) fluted tart tins. Refrigerate for 15 minutes. Prick and bake for 12–15 minutes. Allow to cool. Remove from the tins and place on a baking tray.

3 To make the filling, let the ice cream soften slightly without melting. Dissolve the coffee in a little hot water and stir into the ice cream. Divide the filling between the cases, smooth and freeze until firm.

4 To make the topping, beat the egg whites in a clean, dry bowl until stiff, then add the sugar gradually, beating until thick and glossy. In a separate small bowl, beat the cream until soft peaks form. Fold the cream and egg white mixture together gently.

5 Spoon the topping over the ice cream and sprinkle with drinking chocolate or ground cinnamon. Freeze until the topping is firm. Leave the tarts to stand at room temperature for about 10 minutes before serving.

Espresso Chocolate Tart

serves 12

SWEET SHORTCRUST PASTRY
160 g (5³/4 oz/1¹/3 cups) plain (all-purpose) flour, sifted
2 tablespoons finely ground coffee beans
85 g (3 oz/²/3 cup) icing (confectioners') sugar, sifted
100 g (3¹/2 oz) unsalted butter, chopped
1 egg yolk

50 g (1³/4 oz) dark chocolate, chopped
400 g (14 oz) milk chocolate, chopped
300 ml (10¹/2 fl oz) thick (double/heavy) cream

1 Put the flour, coffee, icing sugar, butter and a pinch of salt in the food processor. Using the pulse button, process until the mixture resembles coarse breadcrumbs.

2 Combine the egg yolk with 1 tablespoon of iced water in a small bowl. Add to the flour mixture and, using the pulse button, process until a dough forms, being careful not to overprocess. If the dough is dry and not coming together, add a little more water, 1 teaspoon at a time. Turn out onto a lightly floured work surface and press the dough into a flat, round disc. Cover with plastic wrap and refrigerate for 30 minutes.

3 Preheat the oven to 200°C (400°F/Gas 6). Grease a 35 x 11 cm (14 x 4¹/4 inch) loose-based rectangular shallow tart tin.

4 Roll out the pastry on a floured work surface until 3 mm (¹/8 inch) thick, to fit the base and sides of the tin. Roll the pastry around the

pin, then lift and ease it into the tin, pressing to fit into the corners. Trim the edges, cover with plastic wrap and refrigerate for 1 hour.

5 Line the pastry shell with a crumpled piece of baking paper and cover the base with baking beads or uncooked rice. Bake the pastry for 10 minutes, then remove the paper and beads and bake for a further 10 minutes, or until the pastry is golden.

6 Put the dark chocolate in a small heatproof bowl. Set the bowl over a small saucepan of simmering water. Stir frequently until the chocolate has melted and the mixture is smooth. Brush the base of the pastry with melted chocolate.

7 Put the milk chocolate and cream in a small heatproof bowl. Set the bowl over a small saucepan of simmering water. Stir until the chocolate has melted and the mixture is smooth. Allow the chocolate to cool slightly, then pour into the tart case. Refrigerate overnight, or until the chocolate filling has set.

Chocolate Fudge Puddings

Serves 8

150 g (5$^{1}/_{2}$ oz) unsalted butter

185 g (6$^{1}/_{2}$ oz/$^{3}/_{4}$ cup) caster (superfine) sugar

100 g (3$^{1}/_{2}$ oz) dark chocolate, melted and cooled

2 eggs

60 g (2$^{1}/_{4}$ oz/$^{1}/_{2}$ cup) plain (all-purpose) flour

125 g (4$^{1}/_{2}$ oz/1 cup) self-raising flour

30 g (1 oz/$^{1}/_{4}$ cup) unsweetened cocoa powder

1 teaspoon bicarbonate of soda (baking soda)

125 ml (4 fl oz/$^{1}/_{2}$ cup) milk

SAUCE

50 g (1$^{3}/_{4}$ oz) unsalted butter, chopped

125 g (4$^{1}/_{2}$ oz) dark chocolate, chopped

125 ml (4 fl oz/$^{1}/_{2}$ cup) cream (whipping)

1 teaspoon natural vanilla extract

1 Preheat the oven to 180°C (350°F/Gas 4). Lightly grease eight 250 ml (9 fl oz/1 cup) pudding moulds with melted butter and line each base with a round of baking paper.

2 Beat the butter and caster sugar until light and creamy. Add the melted chocolate, beating well. Add the eggs one at a time, beating well after each addition.

3 Sift together the plain and self-raising flours, cocoa powder and bicarbonate of soda, then fold into the chocolate mixture. Add the milk and fold through. Half-fill the moulds. Cover the moulds with pieces of greased foil and put in a large, deep ovenproof dish. Pour in

enough boiling water to come halfway up the sides of the moulds. Bake for 35–40 minutes, or until a skewer inserted into the centre of each pudding comes out clean.

4 To make the sauce, combine the butter, chocolate, cream and vanilla in a pan. Stir over low heat until the butter and chocolate have melted. Pour over the pudding and serve with whipped cream.

Chocolate Bread and Butter Pudding

Serves 4-6

60 g (2¹/₄ oz) unsalted butter
6 slices fruit-loaf bread
125 ml (4 fl oz/¹/₂ cup) milk
500 ml (17 fl oz/2 cups) thickened (whipping) cream
115 g (4 oz/¹/₂ cup) caster (superfine) sugar
100 g (3¹/₂ oz) dark chocolate, chopped
4 eggs, lightly beaten
90 g (3¹/₄ oz/¹/₂ cup) dark chocolate chips
2 tablespoons golden or maple syrup

1 Preheat the oven to 160°C (315°F/Gas 2–3). Grease a 1 litre (35 fl oz/4-cup) capacity ovenproof dish. Spread the butter on the bread. Cut the bread into diagonal quarters. Put the bread in the dish in a single layer, overlapping it.

2 Combine the milk, cream and sugar in a saucepan, and stir over low heat until sugar dissolves. Bring to boil, then remove from the heat. Add the chocolate. Stir the mixture until melted and smooth. Cool slightly, then gradually whisk in eggs.

3 Pour half the custard mixture over the bread. Stand for 10 minutes, or until bread absorbs most of the liquid. Pour over the remaining custard mixture. Sprinkle with the chocolate chips. Drizzle with the golden syrup. Bake for 40–45 minutes, or until set and slightly puffed and golden. Serve warm or cold with cream or ice cream.

 This pudding is best eaten on the day it is made.

Caramel Banana Pudding

Serves 6

30 g (1 oz) unsalted butter, softened

6 slices day-old white bread, crusts removed

2 large bananas, peeled and cut into 1 cm (1/2 inch) cubes

3 tablespoons soft brown sugar

1 tablespoon malted milk powder

1 tablespoon caramel corn syrup

3 eggs, lightly beaten

185 ml (6 fl oz/3/4 cup) cream (whipping)

250 ml (9 fl oz/1 cup) milk

1 tablespoon malted milk powder, extra

1. Preheat oven to 180°C (350°F/Gas 4). Lightly grease a shallow 2 litre (70 fl oz/8 cup) capacity, rectangular ovenproof dish with melted butter. Butter the bread and cut 3 slices into rectangles to line the base of dish. Put the banana on top.

2. Combine 2 tablespoons of the sugar, the milk powder, syrup, eggs, cream and milk in a bowl. Whisk until well combined. Pour the mixture over the banana and bread.

3. Cut the remaining bread into 2 cm (3/4 inch) cubes. Put in a bowl with the extra milk powder and remaining sugar. Stir and sprinkle over the pudding. Bake for 45 minutes, or until the custard is set and a skewer inserted in the centre comes out clean. Serve hot or cold with extra cream.

Chocolate Fudge Pecan Pie

Serves 6

PASTRY

155 g (5¹/₂ oz/1¹/₄ cups) plain (all-purpose) flour

2 tablespoons unsweetened cocoa powder

2 tablespoons soft brown sugar

100 g (3¹/₂ oz) unsalted butter, chilled and cubed

200 g (7 oz/2 cups) pecans, roughly chopped

100 g (3¹/₂ oz) dark chocolate, chopped

95 g (3¹/₄ oz/¹/₂ cup) soft brown sugar

170 ml (5¹/₂ fl oz/²/₃ cup) light or dark corn syrup

3 eggs, lightly beaten

2 teaspoons natural vanilla extract

1 Grease a 23 x 18 x 3 cm (9 x 7 x 1¹/₄ inch) pie dish. Sift the flour, cocoa and sugar into a bowl and rub in the butter with your fingertips until the mixture resembles fine breadcrumbs. Make a well, add 2–3 tablespoons of water and mix with a knife, adding more water if necessary.

2 Gather the dough together and lift onto a sheet of baking paper. Press the dough into a disc and refrigerate for 20 minutes. Roll out the pastry between two sheets of baking paper to fit the dish. Line the dish and trim the edges. Refrigerate for 20 minutes.

3 Preheat the oven to 180°C (350°F/Gas 4). Cover the pastry with crumpled baking paper and fill with baking beads or rice. Bake for 15 minutes, then remove the paper and beads and bake for 15–20 minutes, or until the base is dry. Cool completely.

4 Put the pie dish on a flat baking tray to catch any drips. Spread the pecans and chocolate over the pastry base. Combine the sugar, corn syrup, eggs and vanilla in a jug and whisk together with a fork. Pour into the pastry shell, and bake for 45 minutes (the filling will still be a bit wobbly, but will set on cooling). Cool before cutting to serve.

 This pie is best eaten on the day it is made.

Chocolate Meringue Tart

Serves 8

125 g (4¹/2 oz/1 cup) self-raising flour
125 g (4¹/2 oz/1 cup) plain (all-purpose) flour
115 g (4 oz/¹/2 cup) caster (superfine) sugar
125 g (4¹/2 oz) unsalted butter, roughly chopped
1 egg yolk

FILLING
500 g (1 lb 2 oz) ricotta cheese
115 g (4 oz/¹/2 cup) caster (superfine) sugar
30 g (1 oz/¹/4 cup) unsweetened cocoa powder
1 egg yolk
2 eggs
125 g (4¹/2 oz/¹/2 cup) light sour cream

MERINGUE
2 egg whites
55 g (2 oz/¹/4 cup) caster (superfine) sugar
¹/4 teaspoon natural vanilla extract

1 Preheat the oven to 180°C (350°F/Gas 4). Sift together the flours, add the caster sugar, then rub in the butter until the mixture resembles fine breadcrumbs. Combine the egg yolk and 2 tablespoons of water and mix to a firm dough. Knead lightly on a floured surface. Cover and leave for 30 minutes.

2 Roll out the pastry and line a 23 cm (9 inch) tart dish. Prick the base with a fork and bake for 15 minutes. Remove from the oven and allow to cool.

3   Beat the cheese using electric beaters until smooth. Gradually beat in the caster sugar and the cocoa. Add the egg yolk and eggs, beat well, then beat in the sour cream. Pour into the pastry case and bake for 1 hour.

4   To make the meringue, beat the egg whites until soft peaks form. Gradually beat in the sugar and beat until stiff peaks form. Mix in the vanilla extract.

5   Spoon the meringue over the filling and swirl into peaks. Return to the oven and bake for a further 10 minutes. Serve warm or cold with whipped cream.

Chocolate Ricotta Tart

serves 8–10

185 g (6¹/2 oz/1¹/2 cups) plain (all-purpose) flour
100 g (3¹/2 oz) unsalted butter, chopped
2 tablespoons caster (superfine) sugar

FILLING
1.25 kg (2 lb 12 oz) ricotta cheese
125 g (4 oz/¹/2 cup) caster (superfine) sugar
2 tablespoons plain (all-purpose) flour
1 teaspoon instant coffee powder
125 g (4¹/2 oz) chocolate, finely chopped
4 egg yolks

40 g (1¹/2 oz) chocolate, extra
¹/2 teaspoon vegetable oil

1 To make the sweet shortcrust pastry, sift the flour into a large bowl and add the butter. Rub the butter into the flour with your fingertips, until fine and crumbly. Stir in the sugar. Add 3 tablespoons of cold water and mix to form a dough, adding a little more water if necessary. Turn out onto a lightly floured surface and gather together into a ball. Lightly grease a 25 cm (10 inch) round spring-form cake tin. Roll out the dough, then line the tin so that the pastry comes about two-thirds of the way up the side. Cover and refrigerate while making the filling. Preheat the oven to 180°C (350°F/Gas 4).

2 To make the filling, mix together the ricotta, sugar, flour and a pinch of salt until smooth. Dissolve the coffee in 2 teaspoons of hot water. Stir into the ricotta mixture, with the chocolate and egg yolks, until

well mixed. Spoon into the chilled pastry shell and smooth. Chill for 30 minutes, or until firm.

3 Put the spring-form cake tin on a baking tray. Bake for 1 hour, or until firm. Turn off the oven and leave to cool with the door ajar. The tart may crack slightly but this will not be noticeable when it cools and has been decorated.

4 Melt the extra chocolate and stir in the oil. With a fork, flick thin drizzles of melted chocolate over the tart, or pipe over for a neater finish. Cool completely before cutting into wedges for serving.

Caramel Bread Pudding

Serves 6–8

160 g (5¹/₂ oz/²/₃ cup) caster (superfine) sugar
500 g (1 lb 2 oz) panettone or brioche
125 g (4¹/₂ oz/¹/₂ cup) caster (superfine) sugar, extra
500 ml (17 fl oz/2 cups) milk
2 wide strips lemon zest, white pith removed
3 eggs, lightly beaten
thick (double/heavy) cream, to serve

1　Preheat the oven to 180°C (350°F/Gas 4). Lightly grease a 23 x 13 x 7 cm (9 x 5 x 2³/₄ inch) loaf tin.

2　Put the caster sugar with 2 tablespoons of water in a small saucepan over medium heat and stir, without boiling, until the sugar has completely dissolved. Bring to the boil, reduce the heat slightly and simmer, without stirring, for about 10 minutes, or until the syrup becomes a rich golden colour. Pour into the loaf tin and allow to cool.

3　Using a large serrated knife, cut the panettone or brioche into 2 cm (³/₄ inch) thick slices and remove the crusts. Trim into large pieces to fit the tin in three layers, filling any gaps with panettone cut to size.

4　Stir the extra caster sugar, milk and lemon zest in a saucepan over low heat until the sugar has dissolved. Bring to the boil, remove from the heat and transfer to a jug to allow the lemon flavour to be absorbed and the mixture to cool. Remove the lemon zest and whisk in the beaten eggs. Pour the mixture gradually into the tin, allowing it to soak into the panettone after each addition. Set aside for 20 minutes to let the panettone soak up the liquid.

5 Put the loaf tin into a large ovenproof dish and pour in enough hot water to come halfway up the sides of the tin. Bake the pudding for 50 minutes, or until just set. Carefully remove the tin from the baking dish and set aside to cool. Refrigerate the pudding overnight.

6 When ready to serve, turn out onto a plate and cut into slices. Serve with cream.

Caramel, Macadamia and Coconut Pudding

Serves 4-6

140 g (5 oz/3/4 cup lightly packed) soft brown sugar
60 ml (2 fl oz/1/4 cup) cream (whipping)
60 g (2 1/4 oz) butter, melted
135 g (4 3/4 oz/1 cup) chopped macadamia nuts
30 g (1 oz/1/2 cup) shredded coconut
90 g (3 1/4 oz) butter
125 g (4 1/2 oz/1/2 cup) caster (superfine) sugar
2 eggs, lightly beaten
1 teaspoon natural vanilla extract
125 g (4 1/2 oz/1 cup) self-raising flour
80 ml (2 3/4 fl oz/1/3 cup) milk

1 Preheat the oven to 180°C (350°F/Gas 4). Lightly grease a 20 cm (8 inch) round, deep ovenproof dish with melted butter. Line the base with baking paper. Combine the brown sugar, cream and melted butter and pour into the dish. Place the nuts and coconut on a baking tray and toast in the oven for 3–5 minutes, or until golden brown, stirring frequently. Sprinkle over the mixture in the dish.

2 Beat the butter and sugar until light and creamy. Gradually add the eggs and vanilla, beating well after each addition. Fold in the sifted flour alternately with the milk. Spoon into the dish.

3 Bake for 45–50 minutes, or until a skewer inserted into the middle of the pudding comes out clean. Turn out and serve.

Self-Saucing Chocolate Pudding

Serves 4-6

125 g (4¹/2 oz/1 cup) self-raising flour
40 g (1¹/2 oz/¹/3 cup) unsweetened cocoa powder
310 g (11 oz/1¹/3 cups) caster (superfine) sugar
125 ml (4 fl oz/¹/2 cup) milk
1 egg
60 g (2¹/4 oz) unsalted butter, melted
1 teaspoon natural vanilla extract
icing (confectioners') sugar, for dusting

ORANGE CREAM
315 ml (10³/4 fl oz/1¹/4 cups) cream (whipping)
1 teaspoon grated orange zest
1 tablespoon icing (confectioners') sugar
1 tablespoon Grand Marnier

1 Preheat the oven to 180°C (350°F/Gas 4). Lightly grease a 2 litre (70 fl oz/8 cup) ovenproof dish.

2 Sift the flour and 2 tablespoons of the cocoa into a bowl. Stir in 125 g (4¹/2 oz/¹/2 cup) of the sugar. Add the combined milk, egg, butter and vanilla. Pour into the dish. Dissolve the remaining cocoa and sugar in 600 ml (21 fl oz/2¹/2 cups) of boiling water. Pour over the back of a spoon over the pudding mixture. Bake the pudding for 40 minutes, or until a skewer inserted into the centre comes out clean.

3 To make the orange cream, beat all the ingredients until soft peaks form. Dust the pudding with icing sugar and serve with the cream.

Pecan Coffee Tarts

Makes 6

185 g (6^1/2 oz/1^1/2 cups) plain (all-purpose) flour
60 g (2^1/4 oz) icing (confectioners') sugar
125 g (4^1/2 oz) unsalted butter, chopped
60 g (2^1/4 oz/^{1}/2 cup) toasted pecans, finely chopped
1 egg yolk

FILLING
125 g (4^1/2 oz) unsalted butter
90 g (3^1/4 oz/^{1}/2 cup) soft brown sugar, firmly packed
80 ml (2^1/2 fl oz/^{1}/3 cup) cream (whipping)
60 g (2^1/4 oz/^{1}/2 cup) plain (all-purpose) flour
2 teaspoons instant coffee powder
1–2 tablespoons Kahlua
40 g (1^1/2 oz/^{1}/3 cup) pecans, coarsely chopped
1 tablespoon demerara sugar

1 Sift the flour and icing sugar into a large bowl and rub in the butter.
   Stir through the pecans, then add the egg yolk and a little water, if
   necessary, to form a dough. Cover with plastic wrap and refrigerate
   for 30 minutes. Preheat the oven to 200°C (400°F/Gas 6).

2 Divide the dough into six equal portions. Press each portion into six
   10 cm (4 inch) tart tins. Prick the bases with a fork. Put on a baking
   tray and bake for 12–15 minutes. Allow to cool. Reduce the oven
   temperature to 180°C (350°F/Gas 4).

3 To make the filling, melt the butter and sugar in a saucepan. Stir
   until the sugar has dissolved, bring to the boil and simmer gently for

5 minutes, stirring occasionally. Remove from the heat and beat in the blended cream and flour with a wire whisk. Return to the heat. Bring to the boil and then stir over the heat for 3 minutes. Remove from the heat. Dissolve the coffee in 2 teaspoons of hot water. Add the dissolved coffee and the Kahlua to the cream mixture.

4 Pour the filling into the pastry cases. Sprinkle with pecans and sugar and bake for 10 minutes. Cool slightly before serving.

Chocolate Bavarois Coffee Praline Trifle C

desserts

mel Ice Cream Chocolate Crepes Tiramisu

Rich Chocolate Truffles

Makes about 30

185 ml (6 fl oz/³/4 cup) thick (double/heavy) cream
400 g (14 oz) dark chocolate, grated
70 g (2¹/2 oz) unsalted butter, chopped
2 tablespoons Cointreau
unsweetened dark cocoa powder, for rolling

1 Put the cream in a small saucepan and bring to the boil. Remove from the heat and stir in the chocolate until it is completely melted. Add the butter and stir until melted. Stir in the Cointreau. Transfer to a large bowl. Cover and refrigerate for several hours, or overnight.

2 Quickly roll tablespoons of the mixture into balls, and refrigerate until firm. Roll the balls in the cocoa, shake off any excess and return to the refrigerator. Serve at room temperature.

 The truffle mixture can be made and rolled, up to 2 weeks ahead. You will need to roll the balls in cocoa again before serving.

Biscotti and Coffee Parfait

Serves 4

250 ml (9 fl oz/1 cup) cream (whipping)
1 tablespoon soft brown sugar
1 tablespoon Kahlua
8 scoops coffee ice cream
150 g (5½ oz) almond biscotti, chopped
50 g (1¾ oz/⅓ cup) vienna almonds, chopped

1   Whisk the cream and sugar in a large bowl until thick. Add the
    Kahlua and whisk again until well combined.

2   Put a scoop of the ice cream in each of four parfait glasses or
    375 ml (13 fl oz/1½ cups) glass tumblers. Divide half of the
    chopped biscotti among the glasses, then add 1½ tablespoons
    of the cream mixture.

3   Top with the remaining biscotti, 1½ tablespoons of the cream
    mixture and a final scoop of the ice cream. Sprinkle with the chopped
    almonds and serve immediately.

Belgian Waffles with Caramel Apples

Serves 4

75 g (2¹/₂ oz) unsalted butter

75 g (2¹/₂ oz/¹/₃ cup) soft brown sugar

80 ml (2¹/₂ fl oz/¹/₃ cup) golden or maple syrup

4 small red apples, peeled, cored and each cut into eight wedges

8 ready-made Belgian waffles

thick (double/heavy) cream or ice cream, to serve

1 Put the butter, sugar and golden syrup in a non-stick frying pan and cook over medium heat for 2–3 minutes, or until the butter is melted and the sugar is dissolved. Add the apple and cook for 3–5 minutes, or until the apple is just tender. Reduce the heat and simmer for 2 minutes, or until the sauce is thick and syrupy.

2 Lightly toast the waffles. Put two waffles on each serving plate, top each with four apple wedges, then drizzle with a little of the caramel syrup. Serve the waffles and apple warm with a dollop of thick cream or ice cream.

Cappuccino Mousse

Serves 6

250 g (9 oz) white chocolate, melted
125 g (4¹/₂ oz) unsalted butter, softened
2 eggs, lightly beaten
3 teaspoons powdered gelatine
315 ml (10³/₄ fl oz/1¹/₄ cups) cream (whipping)
3 teaspoons instant coffee powder

1 Stir the chocolate, butter and eggs together in a bowl until smooth. Put 2 tablespoons of water in a small heatproof bowl. Sprinkle evenly with the gelatine and leave to go spongy. Bring a large saucepan filled with about 4 cm (1¹/₂ inches) water to the boil. Remove from the heat and carefully lower the bowl with the gelatine into the water. Stir until dissolved, then cool slightly before stirring into the chocolate mixture. Mix well, then cover and chill for 30 minutes, or until just starting to set.

2 Beat the cream into soft peaks and gently fold into the mousse. Spoon about a third of the mousse into a separate bowl and set aside. Mix the coffee powder with 3 teaspoons of hot water. Allow to cool, then fold into the remaining mousse.

3 Spoon the coffee mousse evenly into six small glasses and smooth the surface. Spoon the white mousse over the top. Cover and refrigerate for several hours, or overnight.

Triple Chocolate Terrine

serves 8–10

150 g (5$^1/2$ oz) milk chocolate, chopped

6 eggs

90 g (3 oz/$^3/4$ cup) icing (confectioners') sugar

60 g (2$^1/4$ oz) unsalted butter

500 ml (17 fl oz/2 cups) cream (whipping)

150 g (5$^1/2$ oz) white chocolate, chopped

2 teaspoons instant coffee powder

3–4 teaspoons dark rum

150 g (5$^1/2$ oz) dark chocolate, chopped

1   Line a 10 x 23 cm (4 x 9 inch) loaf tin with baking paper, extending above the top of the tin. Melt the milk chocolate in a small heatproof bowl set over a saucepan of steaming water. Stir the chocolate until smooth.

2   Separate 2 of the eggs and beat the egg whites until soft peaks form. Gradually beat in 30 g (1 oz/$^1/4$ cup) of the icing sugar until thick and glossy. Beat in the 2 egg yolks and the cooled melted chocolate. Melt 20 g (1 oz) of the butter and beat in.

3   Whip 170 ml (5$^1/2$ fl oz/$^2/3$ cup) of the cream into soft peaks. Fold into the egg white mixture and then spoon into the tin, with the tin tilted on one side lengthways. Put in the freezer on this angle and leave for 1–2 hours, or until just firm.

4   Repeat the same method with the white chocolate. Spoon this mixture into the other side of the tin so that the terrine becomes level. Put the tin flat in the freezer to set.

5   Repeat the same method with the remaining ingredients, folding in the coffee dissolved in 1 tablespoon of water, and the rum, with the dark chocolate. Spoon into the tin and smooth the surface. Freeze for several hours. Turn out onto a serving plate. Cut into thin slices to serve.

This terrine can be made a day ahead. Stored in an airtight container.

Coffee Praline Trifle

Serves 4-6

1 ready-made sponge cake

250 ml (9 fl oz/1 cup) brewed strong hot coffee

4 tablespoons sugar

2 tablespoons whisky or brown rum

3 eggs, separated

1 tablespoon cornflour (cornstarch)

250 ml (9 fl oz/1 cup) milk

125 ml (4 fl oz/^{1}/2 cup) cream (whipping), lightly whipped

PRALINE

275 g (9^3/4 oz/1^1/4 cups) sugar

30 g (1 oz/^{1}/3 cup) flaked almonds

1 Cut the sponge cake into 2 cm (3/4 inch) cubes. Put half the cubes in a serving bowl or parfait glasses. Combine the coffee, 2 tablespoons of the sugar and whisky or rum in a small bowl. Allow to cool. Moisten the cake with a little of the coffee mixture.

2 Whisk the egg yolks, remaining sugar and the cornflour in a heatproof bowl until thick. Heat the milk in saucepan until almost boiling. Remove from the heat. Add the milk gradually to the egg mixture, beating.

3 Return the mixture to the saucepan. Stir over medium heat for 5 minutes, or until the custard boils and thickens. Remove from the heat. Cover with plastic wrap and allow to cool. Beat one egg white until stiff peaks form. Using a metal spoon, fold gently into the combined cream and custard.

4   To make the praline, combine the sugar and 125 ml (4 fl oz/^{1}/2 cup) of water in a saucepan. Stir over medium heat without boiling until the sugar has completely dissolved. Bring to the boil, then reduce the heat slightly. Boil without stirring for 10–15 minutes, or until golden brown. Remove from the heat. Add the almonds. Pour the mixture onto a greased and foil-lined baking tray. Allow to cool. Roughly crush. Stir three-quarters into the custard sauce.

5   To assemble the trifle, spoon portions of the custard sauce onto the cake. Top with the remaining cake. Sprinkle with some of the coffee mixture. Spoon over the remaining custard sauce. Cover and refrigerate for 4 hours. Decorate with the remaining praline.

Coffee Granita

Serves 6

185 g (6^1/$_2$ oz/^{3}/$_4$ cup) caster (superfine) sugar

1^1/$_2$ tablespoons unsweetened cocoa powder

1.25 litres (44 fl oz/5 cups) strong espresso coffee

1   Put the sugar and cocoa powder in a large saucepan, gradually add 125 ml (4 fl oz/^{1}/$_2$ cup) of water and stir over low heat until the sugar dissolves. Bring to the boil, then reduce the heat and simmer for 3 minutes.

2   Remove from the heat and add the coffee. Pour into a shallow metal container or tray and cool. Freeze until partially set, then stir with a fork to distribute the ice crystals evenly. Freeze again until firm.

3   Using a fork, work the granita into fine crystals and return to the freezer for 1 hour before serving. Spoon into glasses to serve.

This mixture is extremely hard when frozen, so should be put into a shallow tray and broken up when partially frozen. It is difficult to break up if frozen in a deep container.

Chocolate Bavarois

Serves 6

200 g (7 oz) dark chocolate, chopped
375 ml (13 fl oz/1^1/2 cups) milk
4 egg yolks
90 g (3^1/4 oz/^{1}/3 cup) caster (superfine) sugar
1 tablespoon powdered gelatine
315 ml (10^3/4 fl oz/1^1/4 cups) cream (whipping)

1 Combine the chocolate and milk in a small saucepan. Stir over low heat until the chocolate has melted and the milk just comes to the boil. Remove from the heat.

2 Beat the egg yolks and sugar in a heatproof until combined. Gradually add the hot chocolate milk, whisking until combined. Return to a clean saucepan and cook over low heat until the mixture thickens enough to coat the back of a wooden spoon. Do not allow to boil. Remove from the heat.

3 Put 2 tablespoons of water in a small heatproof bowl. Sprinkle the gelatine in an even layer over the surface and leave to go spongy. Stir into the hot chocolate mixture until dissolved.

4 Refrigerate until the mixture is cold but not set, stirring occasionally. Beat the cream until soft peaks form. Fold into the chocolate mixture in two batches. Pour into six 250 ml (9 fl oz) glasses and refrigerate for several hours, or overnight.

Roasted Caramel Pears

Serves 6

6 firm, ripe pears
1 lemon
460 g (1 lb/2 cups) caster (superfine) sugar
1 cinnamon stick
40 g (1¹/₂ oz) unsalted butter
1 teaspoon natural vanilla extract

1   Preheat the oven to 160°C (315°F/Gas 2–3). Peel the pears then cut them in half down their lengths, keeping the stems intact. Do not remove the core and seeds. Put in a large bowl and squeeze over the juice of one lemon and toss to combine. Add enough cold water to cover the pears while you prepare the caramel — this will prevent them from browning.

2   Put the sugar in a heavy-based saucepan with 250 ml (9 fl oz/ ¹/₂ cup) of water and stir over a high heat until the sugar dissolves. Add the cinnamon stick and bring to the boil. Allow to boil, until the colour starts to take on a light golden hue. Carefully stir the syrup around to evenly distribute the colour until you have a dark golden caramel with a sweet toffee scent. Do not allow the caramel to burn. Remove the caramel from the heat and add the butter and vanilla, stirring until the butter melts.

3   Remove the pears from the water and put cut-side down on a large baking tray. Pour over the caramel and place in the oven. The caramel will have set slightly but should start to melt again after it has been in the oven for a short while. As soon as it begins to melt, start to

spoon it over the pears then continue to do so every 20–30 minutes for the next 3¹/₂–4 hours.

4 The pears are ready when they are an even colour all the way through and have become quite transparent. Serve them warm, drizzled with caramel and juices.

The pears can be refrigerated in their sauce for up to 4 days. Reheat in a warm oven to serve.

Caramel Mousse

Serves 6

2 tablespoons lemon juice
1 tablespoon powdered gelatine
250 g (9 oz/1 cup) sugar
5 eggs
60 g (2¼ oz/¼ cup) caster (superfine) sugar
220 ml (7½ fl oz) cream (whipping)

1 Put the lemon juice in a small bowl, sprinkle the gelatine in an even layer over the surface and leave it to go spongy. Bring a saucepan filled with about 4 cm (1½ inches) water to the boil, then remove from the heat. Set the bowl with the gelatine over the saucepan and stir until the gelatine has completely dissolved.

2 Put the sugar in a heavy-based saucepan and place over low heat. Melt the sugar, stirring until melted. Increase the heat to high and cook the sugar until it turns to caramel. As soon as it becomes a dark golden brown, plunge the base of the saucepan into a sink of cold water to stop the caramel colouring any further. Return the saucepan to the heat. Add 125 ml (4 fl oz/½ cup) of water, then melt the caramel gently until it is a smooth liquid. Allow to cool slightly.

3 Beat the eggs with the caster sugar until they are fluffy and light. Add the caramel and gelatine and continue beating until well combined. Cool the mixture in the refrigerator, stirring every few minutes. When it begins to thicken, whisk the cream until it reaches soft peaks and fold it into the mixture.

Caramel-glazed Figs

Serves 4

60 g (2¹/₄ oz) unsalted butter
45 g (1¹/₂ oz/¹/₄ cup) soft brown sugar
6 fresh figs, halved
thick (heavy/double) cream or ice cream, to serve

1 To make the caramel sauce, put the butter and sugar in a small saucepan and stir for 2–3 minutes, or until the butter has melted and the sugar dissolved.

2 Brush some of the caramel sauce over the cut side of the figs. Grill (broil) for 3–5 minutes, or until soft, brushing with the remaining caramel during cooking. Serve with any remaining sauce and a dollop of thick cream or ice cream.

Mocha Waffles with Espresso Syrup

Makes 8 waffles

ESPRESSO SYRUP

185 g (6^1/$_2$ oz/^{3}/$_4$ cup) caster (superfine) sugar

125 ml (4 fl oz/^{1}/$_2$ cup) brewed espresso coffee

60 ml (2 fl oz/^{1}/$_4$ cup) cream (whipping)

250 g (9 oz/2 cups) plain (all-purpose) flour

40 g (1^1/$_2$ oz/^{1}/$_3$ cup) unsweetened cocoa powder, plus extra for dusting

2 teaspoons baking powder

^{1}/$_2$ teaspoon salt

315 ml (10^3/$_4$ fl oz/1^1/$_4$ cups) milk

2 tablespoons coffee and chicory essence

125 g (4^1/$_2$ oz/^{1}/$_2$ cup) caster (superfine) sugar

3 eggs, separated

60 g (2^1/$_4$ oz) unsalted butter, melted

whipped cream, to serve

1 To make the espresso syrup, put the sugar, coffee, cream and 60 ml (2 fl oz/^{1}/$_4$ cup) of water in a saucepan. Bring to the boil, reduce the heat and simmer for 4–5 minutes. Set aside to cool.

2 Preheat the waffle iron. Sift the flour, cocoa, baking powder and salt into a large bowl. Add the milk, essence, sugar, egg yolks and butter and whisk until smooth. In a clean, dry bowl, beat the egg whites until firm peaks form. Using a large metal spoon, stir a tablespoon of egg white into the batter to loosen it up, then gently fold in the remainder.

3 Brush the waffle iron with melted butter. Pour about 125 ml (4 fl oz/½ cup) batter (the amount will vary according to your waffle iron) into the centre of the iron and spread almost to the corners of the grid. Cook for about 4–5 minutes, or until crisp and golden. Keep warm while cooking the remaining batter. Spoon espresso syrup over the waffles. Dust with cocoa powder and serve with whipped cream.

Chocolate Chestnut Log

serves 10–12

150 g (5^1/$_2$ oz) unsalted butter

80 g (2^3/$_4$ oz/^{1}/$_3$ cup) caster (superfine) sugar

250 ml (9 fl oz/1 cup) tinned chestnut purée

175 g (6 oz) dark chocolate, chopped

60 ml (2 fl oz/^{1}/$_4$ cup) brewed espresso coffee

60 ml (2 fl oz/^{1}/$_4$ cup) brandy

125 g (4^1/$_2$ oz/^{3}/$_4$ cup) almonds

110 g (3^3/$_4$ oz/^{1}/$_2$ cup) sugar

1   Line a loaf tin with plastic wrap. Cream together the butter and sugar until light and creamy. Mix in the purée. Put the chocolate, coffee and brandy in a heatproof bowl and set over a saucepan of simmering water. Stir until the chocolate has melted. Allow to cool. Add to the chestnut mixture and mix well. Spoon into the loaf tin. Freeze overnight.

2   Cover a baking tray with non-stick baking paper. Put the almonds and sugar in a heavy-based frying pan over low heat — tilt the pan but don't stir. The sugar will form lumps then melt to a caramel colour (praline burns quickly so you may need to lift it from the heat occasionally). Pour onto the tray and leave to set. Process, chop or grind with a rolling pin.

3   Cut the chocolate mixture in half lengthways. Wrap each half tightly in plastic wrap and roll to make logs. Freeze for a further 30 minutes. Unwrap and roll in the praline to evenly coat. Cut into slices to serve.

Chocolate Mint Mousse

Serves 4

200 g (7 oz) dark chocolate, chopped
310 ml (10³/₄ fl oz/1¹/₄ cups) thick (double/heavy) cream
8 mint chocolates, chopped

1 Put the chocolate in a small heatproof bowl and set over a saucepan of simmering water. Stir until the chocolate has melted and mixture is smooth. Allow to cool slightly.

2 Using electric beaters, beat the cream until stiff peaks form. Add the melted chocolate to the cream with the after-dinner mints. Stir until combined.

3 Divide among four serving glasses. Refrigerate for 1 hour, or until firm.

Chocolate Crepes with Chocolate Sauce

Makes 8–10

60 g (2¹/4 oz/¹/2 cup) plain (all-purpose) flour

1 tablespoon unsweetened cocoa powder

2 eggs

250 ml (9 fl oz/1 cup) milk

2 tablespoons caster (superfine) sugar

3 oranges

SAUCE

160 g (5³/4 oz) dark chocolate, chopped

185 ml (6 fl oz/³/4 cup) cream (whipping)

125 g (4¹/2 oz/¹/2 cup) sour cream or crème fraîche

75 g (2¹/2 oz) white chocolate, grated

250 g (9 oz/1²/3 cups) blueberries

1 Sift the flour and cocoa into a large bowl and make a well. Gradually whisk in the combined eggs, milk and sugar until the batter is smooth and free of lumps. Transfer to a jug, cover with plastic wrap and set aside for 30 minutes. Cut a 1 cm (¹/2 inch) slice from the ends of each orange. Cut the skin away in a circular motion, cutting only deep enough to remove all the white membrane and skin. Cut the flesh into segments between each membrane. (Do this over a bowl to catch any juice.) Put the segments in a bowl with the juice. Cover with plastic wrap and refrigerate.

2 Heat a 20 cm (8 inch) crepe pan or non-stick frying pan over medium heat and brush lightly with melted butter. Pour 2–3 tablespoons of the crepe batter into the pan and swirl evenly over the base. Cook over medium heat for 1 minute, or until the underside is cooked. Turn the crepe over and cook the other side. Transfer to a plate and cover with a tea towel (dish towel). Repeat with the remaining batter, greasing the pan when necessary. Stack the crepes between greaseproof paper to prevent them sticking together.

3 To make the sauce, drain the oranges and reserve the juice. Combine the juice in a saucepan with the chocolate and cream. Stir over low heat until the chocolate has melted and the mixture is smooth.

4 To assemble the crepes, put a heaped teaspoon of sour cream or crème fraîche on a quarter of each crepe. Sprinkle with the grated white chocolate. Fold the crepe in half, and in half again to make a wedge shape. Put two crepes on each serving plate. Spoon the warm sauce over the crepes and serve with the orange segments and blueberries.

Coffee Cremets with Chocolate Sauce

Serves 4

250 g (9 oz) cream cheese
250 ml (9 fl oz/1 cup) thick (double/heavy) cream
80 ml (2^1/2 fl oz/^{1}/3 cup) brewed coffee
80 g (2^3/4 oz/^{1}/3 cup) caster (superfine) sugar

CHOCOLATE SAUCE
100 g (3^1/2 oz) dark chocolate
50 g (1^3/4 oz) unsalted butter

1 Line four 100 ml (3^1/2 fl oz) ramekins or heart-shaped moulds with muslin, leaving enough muslin hanging over the side to wrap over the cremet.

2 Beat the cream cheese until smooth, then whisk in the cream. Add the coffee and sugar and mix together. Spoon into the ramekins and fold the muslin over the top. Refrigerate for at least 1^1/2 hours. Unwrap the muslin and turn the cremets out onto individual plates, carefully peeling off the muslin each one.

3 To make the chocolate sauce, gently melt the chocolate in a saucepan with the butter and 80 ml (2^1/2 fl oz/^{1}/3 cup) of water. Stir well to make a shiny sauce, then allow to cool slightly. Pour a little chocolate sauce over each cremet.

Tiramisu

Serves 6-8

750 ml (26 fl oz/3 cups) brewed coffee, cooled

60 ml (2 fl oz/¼ cup) brandy or Kahlua

2 eggs, separated

60 g (2¼ oz/¼ cup) caster (superfine) sugar

250 g (9 oz) mascarpone cheese

250 ml (9 fl oz/1 cup) cream (whipping), whipped

16 large savoiardi (lady fingers)

2 teaspoons unsweetened dark cocoa powder

1   Put the coffee and liqueur in a bowl. Using electric beaters, beat the egg yolks and sugar in a small bowl for 3 minutes, or until thick and pale. Add the mascarpone and beat until just combined. Fold in the cream with a metal spoon.

2   Beat the egg whites until soft peaks form. Fold quickly and lightly into the cream mixture with a metal spoon, trying not to reduce the volume.

3   Quickly dip half the biscuits, one at a time, into the coffee mixture. Drain off any excess and arrange the biscuits in the base of a deep serving dish. Spread half the cream mixture over the biscuits.

4   Dip the remaining biscuits into the coffee mixture and repeat the layers. Smooth the surface and dust liberally with cocoa powder. Refrigerate for 2 hours, or until firm.

White Chocolate Fondue

serves 6–8

125 ml (4 fl oz/^{1}/$_2$ cup) light corn syrup
170 ml (5^1/$_2$ fl oz/^{2}/$_3$ cup) thick (double/heavy) cream
60 ml (2 fl oz/^{1}/$_4$ cup) Cointreau
250 g (9 oz) white chocolate, chopped
marshmallows and chopped fresh fruit, for serving

1 Combine the corn syrup and cream in a small saucepan or fondue.
   Bring to the boil, then remove from the heat.

2 Add the Cointreau and white chocolate and stir until melted. Serve
   with marshmallows and fresh fruit.

Dark Chocolate Fondue

Serves 6-8

250 g (9 oz) dark chocolate, chopped
125 ml (4 fl oz/½ cup) thick (double/heavy) cream
marshmallows and chopped fresh fruit, for serving

1 Put the chocolate and cream in a fondue or a heatproof bowl and set over a saucepan of water which has been brought to the boil and then taken off the heat. Serve with marshmallows and fresh fruit.

Fruits which work well in fondues include strawberries, pears, cherries and bananas.

Chocolate Eclairs

Makes 18

125 g (4¹/2 oz) unsalted butter
125 g (4¹/2 oz/1 cup) plain (all-purpose) flour, sifted
4 eggs, lightly beaten
300 ml (10¹/2 fl oz) cream (whipping), whipped
150 g (5¹/2 oz) dark chocolate, chopped

1 Preheat the oven to 210°C (415°F/Gas 6–7). Grease two baking trays. Combine the butter and 250 ml (9 fl oz/1 cup) water in a large heavy-based saucepan. Stir over medium heat until the butter melts. Increase the heat, bring to the boil, then remove from the heat.

2 Add the flour to the saucepan and quickly beat into the water with a wooden spoon. Return to the heat and continue beating until the mixture leaves the side of the pan and forms a ball. Transfer to a large bowl and cool slightly. Beat the mixture to release any remaining heat. Gradually add the egg. Beat well after each addition until all the egg has been added and the mixture is glossy.

3 Spoon the mixture into a piping bag fitted with a 1.5 cm (⁵/8 inch) plain nozzle. Sprinkle the baking trays lightly with water. Pipe 15 cm (6 inch) lengths onto the trays, leaving room for expansion. Bake for 10–15 minutes. Reduce the heat to 180°C (350°F/Gas 4). Bake for a further 15 minutes, or until golden and firm. Cool on a wire rack. Split each eclair, removing any uncooked dough. Fill the puffs with cream.

4 Put the chocolate in a heatproof bowl and set over a saucepan of simmering water. Stir occasionally until the chocolate has melted. Spread over the tops of the eclairs.

Chocolate Chip Pancakes

Makes 16

250 g (9 oz/2 cups) self-raising flour

2 tablespoons unsweetened cocoa powder

1 teaspoon bicarbonate of soda (baking soda)

60 g (2 oz/^{1}/4 cup) caster (superfine) sugar

130 g (4^1/2 oz/^{3}/4 cup) dark chocolate chips

250 ml (9 fl oz/1 cup) milk

250 ml (9 fl oz/1 cup) cream

2 eggs, lightly beaten

30 g (1 oz) unsalted butter, melted

3 egg whites

whipped cream or ice cream, to serve

chocolate fudge sauce (see page 209), to serve

1   Combine the flour, cocoa, bicarbonate of soda, sugar and chocolate chips in a bowl. Make a well in the centre. Whisk together the milk, cream, eggs and melted butter. Stir into the flour mixture until just combined. Cover and set aside for 15 minutes.

2   Beat the egg whites in a clean, dry bowl until soft peaks form. Using a metal spoon, stir a heaped tablespoon of the beaten egg white into the batter, then fold in the remaining egg white until combined.

3   Heat a frying pan and brush with melted butter. Pour 60 ml (2 fl oz/ ^{1}/4 cup) of batter into the pan. Cook over medium heat until the underside is browned. Flip the pancake over and cook the other side. Transfer to a plate and cover with a tea towel (dish towel) while cooking the remaining batter. Serve the pancakes with whipped cream or ice cream and drizzle with warm chocolate fudge sauce.

Mocha Ice Cream

Serves 4-6

40 g (1¹/4 oz/¹/2 cup) espresso coffee beans
750 ml (26 fl oz/3 cups) cream (whipping)
250 g (9 oz) dark cooking chocolate, chopped
185 g (6¹/2 oz/³/4 cup) caster (superfine) sugar
6 egg yolks
250 ml (9 fl oz/1 cup) milk

1   Line a rectangular tin with plastic wrap and freeze. Combine the coffee beans and cream in a saucepan. Stir over medium heat until the mixture just starts to boil. Add the chocolate, remove from the heat and set aside for 1 minute before stirring.

2   Combine the sugar and egg yolks in a large bowl, whisk until slightly thickened, then whisk in the milk. Gradually add the coffee mixture with the beans and whisk until smooth. Strain the mixture and discard the beans.

3   Return the mixture to the saucepan and stir over low heat until the mixture thickens. Do not boil. Remove from the heat and set aside to cool.

4   Put the mixture into the prepared tin and freeze until just firm. Transfer to a large chilled bowl and beat with electric beaters until thick. Return to the tin and cover with plastic wrap and freeze again until firm. Repeat, beating once more before transferring to a container for storage in the freezer. Cover the surface with plastic wrap or baking paper.

Chocolate Meringue Kisses

Makes 25

2 egg whites
115 g (4 oz/^{1}/2 cup) caster (superfine) sugar
^{1}/4 teaspoon ground cinnamon

FILLING
125 g (4^1/2 oz) dark chocolate chips
90 g (3^1/4 oz/^{1}/3 cup) sour cream

1   Preheat the oven to 150°C (300°F/Gas 2). Line two baking trays with baking paper.

2   Using electric beaters, beat the egg whites in a bowl until soft peaks form. Gradually add the sugar, beating well after each addition. Beat until the sugar has dissolved and mixture is thick and glossy. Add the cinnamon and beat until just combined.

3   Transfer the mixture to a piping bag fitted with a 1 cm (^{1}/2 inch) fluted tube. Pipe stars of 1.5 cm (^{5}/8 inch) diameter onto prepared trays 3 cm (1^1/4 inches) apart. Bake for 30 minutes, or until pale and crisp. Cool in the oven with the door ajar.

4   To make the filling, put the chocolate and sour cream in a small heatproof bowl and set over a saucepan of simmering water. Stir until the chocolate has melted. Remove from the heat. Cool slightly. Sandwich the meringues together with the filling. Serve immediately.

 Unfilled meringues can be made several days ahead. Store in an airtight container, between sheets of baking paper.

Chocolate Mousse

Makes 4

250 g (9 oz) dark chocolate
3 eggs
55 g (2 oz/^{1}/4 cup) caster (superfine) sugar
2 teaspoons dark rum
250 ml (9 fl oz/1 cup) cream (whipping), whipped to soft peaks

1 Put the chocolate in a small heatproof bowl and set over a saucepan of simmering water. Stir until the chocolate has melted and the mixture is smooth. Set aside to cool.

2 Using electric beaters, beat the eggs and sugar in a small bowl for 5 minutes, or until thick and pale.

3 Transfer the mixture to a large bowl. Using a metal spoon, fold the melted chocolate and rum into the egg mixture, then fold in the whipped cream. Work quickly until the mixture is just combined.

4 Spoon the mousse into four 250 ml (9 fl oz/1-cup) capacity ramekins. Refrigerate 2 hours, or until set.

Caramel Ice Cream

Serves 4

70 g (2¹/₂ oz/¹/₃ cup) sugar
80 ml (2¹/₂ fl oz) cream (whipping)
3 egg yolks
360 ml (12 fl oz) milk
1 vanilla pod

1 To make the caramel, put 45 g (1¹/₂ oz) of the sugar in a heavy-based saucepan and heat until it dissolves and starts to caramelize — tip the saucepan from side to side as the sugar cooks to keep the colouring even. Remove from the heat and carefully add the cream. Stir over low heat until the caramel re-melts.

2 Whisk the egg yolks and remaining sugar until light and fluffy. Put the milk and vanilla pod in a saucepan and bring to the boil, then strain over the caramel. Bring back to the boil and pour over the egg yolk mixture, whisking continuously.

3 Pour the custard back into the saucepan and cook, stirring, until thick. Do not let it boil. Pass through a sieve into a bowl and put over ice to allow the mixture to cool quickly.

4 Churn in an ice cream maker following the manufacturer's instructions. Alternatively, pour into a plastic freezer box, cover and freeze. Stir every 30 minutes with a whisk during freezing to break up the ice crystals and give a better texture. Freeze overnight with a layer of plastic wrap over the surface and the lid on the container. Keep in the freezer until ready to serve.

Coffee Meringues with Chocolate Ganache and Dark Chocolate Sauce

Serves 6

MERINGUES
2 egg whites
100 g (3^1/$_2$ oz/^{1}/$_2$ cup) caster (superfine) sugar
^{1}/$_2$ teaspoon coffee and chicory essence

GANACHE
100 ml (3^1/$_2$ fl oz) cream (whipping)
75 g (2^1/$_2$ oz) milk chocolate, chopped

SAUCE
125 ml (4 fl oz/^{1}/$_2$ cup) cream (whipping)
180 g (6^1/$_2$ oz) dark chocolate, chopped

1 tablespoon cream (whipping), to serve

1 Preheat the oven to 150°C (300°F/Gas 2). Line a baking tray with baking paper. Whisk the egg whites in a clean, dry bowl until soft peaks form. Add the sugar, a tablespoon at a time, beating well after each addition until stiff and glossy. Lightly fold in the coffee and chicory essence until just combined.

2 Spoon the meringue into a large piping bag fitted with a large star nozzle. Pipe six individual whirls of meringue onto the lined baking tray. Pipe six flatter whirls for the base. Bake for 20–30 minutes, or until crisp. Turn off the oven and leave the meringues inside for a further 30 minutes to dry out completely. Allow to cool.

3 To make the chocolate ganache, bring the cream to a simmer, then remove from the heat. Stir in the milk chocolate until it has melted and leave to cool. Whisk over a bowl of iced water until just stiff and mousse-like. Pipe or spread some of the mixture onto the flat meringues and put the peaked meringues on top.

4 To make the dark chocolate sauce, put the cream and the dark chocolate in a small saucepan and stir over low heat until the chocolate has melted. Pour a little of the dark chocolate sauce into the centre of each serving plate and spoon a couple of teaspoons of the sauce around the outside. Put a couple of drops of cream on each teaspoon of sauce. Using a skewer, start from the centre of the plate and pull the cream through the sauce. Place a meringue in the middle of the sauce and serve immediately.

Hot Chocolate Soufflé

Serves 6

175 g (6 oz) dark chocolate, chopped
5 egg yolks, lightly beaten
60 g (2¹/₄ oz/¹/₄ cup) caster (superfine) sugar
7 egg whites
icing (confectioners') sugar, for dusting

1 Preheat the oven to 200°C (400°F/Gas 6). Wrap a double layer of baking paper around six 250 ml (9 fl oz/1 cup) ramekins, to come 3 cm (1¹/₄ inches) above the rim. Secure with string. Brush the ramekins with butter and sprinkle with caster sugar. Shake to coat evenly, then tip out excess. Put on a baking tray.

2 Put the chocolate in a heatproof bowl and set over a saucepan of simmering. Stir occasionally until the chocolate has melted. Stir in the egg yolks and sugar. Transfer the mixture to a large bowl.

3 Beat the egg whites in a large bowl until firm peaks form. Fold a third of the beaten egg white through the chocolate mixture to loosen it. Using a metal spoon, fold through the remaining egg white until just combined. Spoon the mixture into the ramekins and bake for 12–15 minutes, or until well risen and just set. Cut the string and remove the collars. Lightly dust with the icing sugar and serve.

Coffee Cream Whip

Serves 4

2 eggs
2 tablespoons caster (superfine) sugar
1 tablespoon instant coffee powder
250 ml (9 fl oz/1 cup) thick (double/heavy) cream
8 savoiardi (lady fingers), roughly chopped
2 tablespoons brandy
unsweetened cocoa powder, for dusting

1　Using electric beaters, beat the eggs and the sugar for 3 minutes or until thick and pale. Dissolve the coffee powder in 2 teaspoons of hot water and add to the mixture with the cream. Beat for 3 minutes, or until soft peaks form.

2　Add the sponge finger biscuits and brandy. Stir until combined. Divide among four serving dishes. Refrigerate for at least 1 hour. Serve dusted with cocoa.

Chocolate Cherry Trifle

Serves 6

350 g (12 oz) ready-made chocolate cake

900 g (2 lb) tinned pitted dark cherries

60 ml (2 fl oz/¼ cup) Kirsch

CUSTARD

2 egg yolks

2 tablespoons sugar

1 tablespoon cornflour (cornstarch)

250 ml (9 fl oz/1 cup) milk

1 teaspoon natural vanilla extract

185 ml (6 fl oz/3/4 cup) cream (whipping), lightly whipped

30 g (1 oz) toasted slivered almonds, to decorate

whipped cream, to serve

1 Cut the cake into thin strips. Line the base of a 1.75 litre (61 fl oz/ 7 cups) serving dish or bowl with one-third of the cake.

2 Drain the cherries, reserving the juice. Combine 250 ml (9 fl oz/ 1 cup) of the juice with the Kirsch and sprinkle some of the syrup over the cake. Spoon some cherries over the cake.

3 To make the custard, whisk the egg yolks, sugar and cornflour in a heatproof bowl until thick and pale. Heat the milk in a saucepan until almost boiling, then remove from the heat. Gradually add to the egg mixture, beating constantly. Return to a clean saucepan and stir over medium heat for 5 minutes, or until thickened. Remove from the

heat and add the vanilla. Cover the surface with plastic wrap. Allow to cool, then fold in the whipped cream.

4   To assemble, spoon a third of the custard over the cherries and cake in the dish. Top with more cake, syrup, cherries and custard. Repeat the layering process, ending with custard on top. Cover and refrigerate for 3–4 hours. Decorate with almonds and whipped cream.

Coffee Gelato

Serves 6

5 egg yolks
125 g (4$^{1}/_{2}$ oz/$^{1}/_{2}$ cup) sugar
500 ml (17 fl oz/2 cups) milk
120 ml (4 fl oz/$^{1}/_{2}$ cup) brewed espresso coffee
1 tablespoon Tia Maria

1   Whisk the egg yolks and half the sugar together until pale and
    creamy. Put the milk, coffee and remaining sugar in a saucepan and
    bring to the boil. Pour over the egg mixture and whisk to combine.
    Return to the saucepan and cook over low heat, stirring continuously
    until the mixture is thick enough to coat the back of a wooden spoon
    — do not allow the custard to boil.

2   Strain the custard into a bowl and cool over ice. Stir in the Tia
    Maria. Churn in an ice cream maker following the manufacturer's
    instructions. Alternatively, pour into a plastic freezer box, cover and
    freeze. Stir every 30 minutes with a whisk during freezing to break up
    the ice crystals and give a better texture. Keep in the freezer until
    ready to serve.

Orange-chocolate Cups

Serves 6

125 g (4$^1/_2$ oz) dark chocolate, finely chopped
375 ml (13 fl oz/1$^1/_2$ cups) milk
5 egg yolks
2 teaspoons finely grated orange zest
90 g (3$^1/_4$ oz/$^1/_3$ cup) caster (superfine) sugar
1 tablespoon powdered gelatine
185 ml (6 fl oz/$^3/_4$ cup) cream (whipping), lightly whipped

1 Warm the chocolate and milk in a saucepan over low heat until the chocolate melts. Whisk the yolks with the zest and sugar until the mixture is light and creamy. Pour the chocolate milk mixture into the egg while stirring, then return the mixture to the saucepan. Stir over low heat until the custard thickens slightly and coats the back of a wooden spoon — do not boil. Remove from the heat, transfer to a bowl, then allow to cool.

2 Put 60 ml (2 fl oz/$^1/_2$ cup) of water in a small heatproof bowl. Sprinkle evenly with the gelatine and leave to go spongy. Bring a large saucepan filled with about 4 cm (1$^1/_2$ inches) of water to the boil. Remove from the heat and lower the bowl with the gelatine into the water. Stir until dissolved. Stir into the warm custard and mix well. Allow to cool.

3 Using a metal spoon, fold in the whipped cream. Pour into six dessert dishes and refrigerate until firm.

Cappuccino Pikelets with Kahlua Cream

Makes 15–20

KAHLUA CREAM
2 teaspoons espresso coffee powder
2 tablespoons caster (superfine) sugar
60 ml (2 fl oz/$1/4$ cup) Kahlua
300 ml ($10^{1}/2$ fl oz) cream, lightly whipped

PIKELETS (FLAPJACKS)
1 tablespoon espresso coffee powder
$1/4$ teaspoon ground cinnamon
250 g (9 oz/2 cups) self-raising flour
95 g ($3^{1}/4$ oz/$1/2$ cup) soft brown sugar
2 eggs
250 ml (9 fl oz/1 cup) milk

strawberries, to serve

1 To make the Kahlua cream, combine the coffee, sugar and Kahlua
in a small saucepan. Stir over low heat until the sugar dissolves. Set
aside to cool. Gradually stir into the cream until smooth. Cover and
refrigerate until ready to serve.

2 Combine the coffee powder and cinnamon in a heatproof bowl and
add 60 ml (2 fl oz/$1/4$ cup) of boiling water. Stir to dissolve and set
aside to cool.

3 Sift the flour into a bowl and stir in the sugar, making a well in the
centre. Whisk the eggs, milk and cooled coffee in a jug and gradually
pour into the well, whisking until just smooth.

4 Heat a frying pan over medium heat and brush lightly with melted
   butter. Drop heaped tablespoons of batter into the pan, allowing
   room for spreading. Cook the pikelets until small bubbles appear on
   the surface and the underside has browned. Turn over and cook the
   other side. Transfer to a plate and cover with a tea towel (dish towel)
   to keep warm while cooking the remaining batter. Serve with the
   Kahlua Cream and strawberries.

Caramel Sticky Rice

Serves 4

400 g (14 oz/2 cups) white glutinous rice
250 ml (9 fl oz/1 cup) coconut milk
85 g (3 oz) palm sugar, grated
whipped cream or ice cream, to serve

1 Put the rice in a sieve and wash until the water runs clear. Put in a glass or ceramic bowl, cover with water and soak for 8 hours. Drain.

2 Line a bamboo steamer with baking paper or a damp tea towel (dish towel) and place over a wok filled with water. Don't let the base of the steamer touch the water. Spread the rice over the paper, fold the paper or tea towel over the rice and cover with another sheet of paper or tea towel. Tuck it in so the rice is completely encased. Cover with the bamboo lid and steam over medium heat for 50 minutes, checking the water regularly, until just cooked.

3 Put the coconut milk, palm sugar and a pinch of salt in a small saucepan and stir until boiling. Reduce the heat and simmer for 15 minutes, or until thick.

4 Pour a quarter of the caramel over the rice, fork it through, cover with the paper and lid and steam for 5 minutes. Repeat with the remaining caramel, cooking until the rice is plump and sticky. Transfer the rice to a metal tray or shallow tin, pressing in lightly, then set aside until firm. Cut into diamonds and serve warm with whipped cream or ice cream.

Chocolate Semifreddo

Serves 10

500 ml (17 fl oz/2 cups) cream (whipping)
150 g (5^1/2 oz/^{2}/3 cup) caster (superfine) sugar
50 g (1^3/4 oz/^{1}/2 cup) unsweetened cocoa powder
4 eggs, separated
60 ml (2 fl oz/^{1}/4 cup) brandy
60 g (2^1/4 oz/^{1}/2 cup) icing (confectioners') sugar
150 g (5^1/2 oz/1 cup) skinned hazelnuts, roughly chopped

1   Line a 1.5 litre (52 fl oz/6 cups) loaf tin with two long strips of foil.
    Heat 200 ml (7 fl oz) of the cream in a small saucepan. Combine the
    caster sugar, cocoa powder and egg yolks in a heatproof bowl, then
    add the hot cream and mix well. Pour the mixture back into the
    saucepan and cook over low heat, stirring continuously, until the
    mixture is thick enough to coat the back of a wooden spoon — do
    not allow to boil. Stir in the brandy and remove from the heat. Cover
    the surface with plastic wrap and cool for 30 minutes.

2   Whisk the egg whites in a clean, dry bowl until stiff peaks form. Whip
    the remaining cream in a large bowl until soft peaks form. Add the
    icing sugar and continue whipping until stiff and glossy. Lightly fold
    the chocolate custard into the whipped cream, then fold in the egg
    whites. Gently fold through the hazelnuts. Spoon into the tin, smooth
    the surface and cover with foil. Freeze for at least 24 hours. Leave at
    room temperature for 5 minutes before cutting in slices to serve.

Baked Chocolate Custards

Serves 10

30 g (1 oz) unsalted butter, melted

55 g (2 oz/¼ cup) caster (superfine) sugar, for dusting

300 ml (10½ fl oz) cream (whipping)

200 ml (7 fl oz) milk

200 g (7 oz) dark chocolate, roughly chopped

grated zest from 1 orange

6 eggs

115 g (4 oz/½ cup) caster (superfine) sugar, extra

raspberries, to serve

icing (confectioners') sugar, for dusting

1. Preheat the oven to 160°C (315°F/Gas 2–3). Grease ten 125 ml (4 fl oz/½ cup) ramekins and dust with sugar.

2. Put the cream and milk in a saucepan over low heat and bring almost to the boil. Add the chocolate and stir over low heat until the chocolate has melted. Stir in the orange zest.

3. Whisk the eggs and sugar in a large bowl for 5 minutes, or until pale and thick. Whisk a little of the hot chocolate cream into the eggs, then pour the egg mixture onto the remaining chocolate cream, whisking continuously.

4. Divide the mixture among the ramekins. Put the custards in a large roasting tin and pour in enough hot water to come halfway up the sides of the ramekins. Cover the tin with foil and bake for 30 minutes, or until the custards are set. Immediately remove the ramekins from the water bath. Set aside to cool completely. Turn out onto a serving dish. Top with the raspberries and dust with icing sugar.

Hot Buttered Caramel Waffles

Serves 2-4

4 ready-made waffles
80 g (2³/4 oz) unsalted butter
80 g (2³/4 oz/¹/3 cup) soft brown sugar
170 ml (5¹/2 fl oz/²/3 cup) cream (whipping)
2 tablespoons rum or brandy
vanilla ice cream, to serve

1 Toast the waffles on each side until golden brown. Heat the butter in a non-stick frying pan. When the butter is foaming, add the waffles, turning quickly to coat in the butter. Remove from the pan and keep the waffles warm in a low oven, taking care not to let them become soggy.

2 Working quickly, sprinkle the sugar into the pan, stirring into the remaining butter. Add the cream and rum. Simmer for 1–2 minutes. Serve the sauce spooned over the buttered waffles with a scoop of ice cream.

Profiteroles with Coffee Mascarpone and Dark Chocolate Sauce

Makes 16

125 g (4 1/2 oz/1 cup) plain (all-purpose) flour
70 g (2 1/2 oz) unsalted butter, cubed
1/2 teaspoon salt
4 eggs, at room temperature

FILLING
2 tablespoons instant coffee powder
225 g (8 oz) mascarpone cheese
2 tablespoons icing (confectioners') sugar

DARK CHOCOLATE SAUCE
100 g (3 1/2 oz) dark chocolate, chopped
20 g (3/4 oz) unsalted butter
80 ml (2 1/2 fl oz/1/3 cup) cream (whipping)

1   Preheat the oven to 200°C (400°F/Gas 6) and lightly grease two
    baking trays. Sift the flour onto a large piece of baking paper. Put the
    butter, salt and 250 ml (9 fl oz/1 cup) of water into a saucepan and
    bring to the boil, stirring occasionally. Using the baking paper as a
    funnel, pour the flour quickly into the boiling mixture. Reduce the
    heat to low, then beat vigorously with a wooden spoon until the
    mixture leaves the side of the pan and forms a smooth ball.

2   Transfer the mixture to a bowl and set aside to cool until lukewarm.
    Using electric beaters, beat in the eggs, one at a time, until
    the mixture is thick and glossy. Using two spoons, gently drop
    16 rounded balls of the mixture about 3 cm (1 1/4 inches) in diameter

and 3 cm (1¼ inches) apart onto the prepared trays. Bake for
20 minutes, or until the balls are puffed. Reduce the oven to 180°C
(350°F/Gas 4) and bake for another 10 minutes, or until the puffs are
golden brown and crisp.

3   Using a small sharp knife, gently slit the puffs to allow the steam to
escape, then return them to the oven for 10 minutes, or until the
insides are dry. Set aside to cool to room temperature.

4   Meanwhile, to make the filling, dissolve the coffee in 1 tablespoon
of boiling water. Set aside to cool. Beat the coffee, mascarpone and
icing sugar until just combined. Be careful not to overmix or the
mascarpone will split.

5   To make the dark chocolate sauce, put the chocolate, butter and
cream in a heatproof bowl set over a saucepan of simmering water.
Stir until combined. Set aside to cool slightly. Just before serving, slit
the profiteroles in half and sandwich together with the filling. Drizzle
with the dark chocolate sauce.

Petits Pots au Chocolat

Serves 8

170 ml (5^1/$_2$ fl oz/^{2}/$_3$ cup) thickened (whipping) cream

^{1}/$_2$ vanilla bean, split lengthways

150 g (5^1/$_2$ oz) dark bittersweet chocolate, chopped

80 ml (2^1/$_2$ fl oz/^{1}/$_3$ cup) milk

2 egg yolks

60 g (2^1/$_4$ oz/^{1}/$_4$ cup) caster (superfine) sugar

whipped cream and unsweetened cocoa powder, to serve

1 Preheat the oven to 140°C (275°F/Gas 1). Lightly brush eight 80 ml (2^1/$_2$ fl oz/^{1}/$_3$ cup) moulds or ramekins with melted butter and put them in a deep baking dish. Heat the cream in a small saucepan with the vanilla bean until the cream is warm, then leave to infuse.

2 Combine the chocolate and milk in a small saucepan. Stir over low heat until the chocolate has just melted.

3 Put the egg yolks in a small bowl, and slowly whisk in the sugar. Continue whisking until the sugar has dissolved and the mixture is light and creamy. Scrape the seeds out of the vanilla bean into the cream, and discard the empty bean. Add the vanilla cream and the melted chocolate mixture to the beaten egg yolks, and mix well.

4 Pour the mixture into the ramekins, filling approximately two-thirds of the way. Fill the baking dish with enough boiling water to come halfway up the pots. Bake for 45 minutes, or until the chocolate pots have puffed up slightly and feel spongy. Remove from the baking dish and cool. Cover with plastic wrap and refrigerate for 6 hours before serving. Serve with cream and dust with cocoa powder.

Individual Coffee Pavlovas with White Chocolate

Serves 6

4 egg whites
220 g (7³/4 oz/1 cup) sugar
1 tablespoon instant coffee powder
185 g (6¹/2 oz) white chocolate, melted
4 egg yolks
185 ml (6 fl oz/³/4 cup) cream (whipping), whipped
250 g (9 oz) strawberries, quartered

1   Preheat the oven to 150°C (300°F/Gas 2). Line two baking sheets with baking paper. Put the egg whites in a large bowl. Using electric beaters, beat the egg whites until soft peaks form. Gradually add the sugar, beating after each addition. Beat 5–10 minutes until thick and glossy and the sugar has dissolved. Dissolve the coffee with 1 teaspoon of water and add to the meringue mixture.

2   Divide the meringue mixture into six portions. Drop each portion 5 cm (2 inches) apart on baking trays. Shape evenly, running a flat-bladed knife around the edge and over the top of the meringue rounds. Smooth the edges with a knife, making mini pavlova shapes. Bake for 45 minutes, or until crisp. Turn off the oven and cool the pavlovas in the oven with the door ajar.

3   Put the chocolate in a bowl. Whisk in the egg yolks and stir until smooth. Fold in the whipped cream. Refrigerate until firm. Spoon the chocolate mixture over each pavlova and top with strawberries.

Sunken Chocolate Desserts

Serves 4

140 g (5 oz/^{2}/$_3$ cup) caster (superfine) sugar

150 g (5^1/$_2$ oz) dark chocolate, chopped

125 g (4^1/$_2$ oz) unsalted butter

3 eggs

30 g (1 oz/^{1}/$_4$ cup) plain (all-purpose) flour

icing (confectioners') sugar, for dusting

ice cream, to serve

1 Preheat the oven to 180°C (350°F/Gas 4). Lightly grease four 250 ml (9 fl oz/1 cup) ramekins and coat lightly with 1 tablespoon of the caster sugar.

2 Put the chocolate and butter in a small heatproof bowl and set over a small saucepan of simmering water. Stir until the chocolate and butter have melted. Remove from the heat.

3 Whisk the eggs and sugar in a heatproof bowl using electric beaters until pale and thick. Sift the flour onto the egg mixture, then whisk the flour into the mixture. Whisk in the melted chocolate.

4 Divide the batter between the prepared ramekins and put on a baking tray. Bake for 30–35 minutes, or until set and firm to the touch. Allow to cool in the ramekins for 10 minutes before turning out onto serving plates. Alternatively, serve them in the ramekins, dusted with icing sugar. Serve warm with ice cream.

Chocolate Affogato

Serves 4

250 g (9 oz) dark chocolate, chopped
1 litre (35 fl oz/4 cups) milk
6 eggs
110 g (3³/4 oz/¹/2 cup) caster (superfine) sugar
340 ml (11¹/2 fl oz/1¹/3 cups) thick (double/heavy) cream
80 ml (2¹/2 fl oz/¹/3 cup) Frangelico
200 ml (7 fl oz) brewed espresso coffee

1 Put the chocolate milk in a saucepan and heat low heat. Stir the mixture until smooth. Do not boil. Whisk the eggs and sugar together in a heatproof bowl using electric beaters until the mixture is pale and frothy. Add the milk and chocolate mixture and the cream, and mix well.

2 Pour the mixture into a shallow plastic or metal container and place in the freezer. Whisk the mixture every hour to break up the ice crystals as they form. When the mixture gets very stiff, leave it to set overnight.

3 Place a scoop of the ice cream in each of the four small cups. Pour over the Frangelico and the hot coffee and serve immediately.

Hot Mocha Soufflé

Serves 20

60 g (2¼ oz/¼ cup) caster (superfine) sugar
40 g (1½ oz) unsalted butter
2 tablespoons plain (all-purpose) flour
185 ml (6 fl oz/¾ cup) milk
1 tablespoon espresso coffee powder
100 g (3½ oz) dark chocolate, melted
4 eggs, separated
icing (confectioners') sugar, for dusting

1 Preheat the oven to 180°C (350°F/Gas 4). Wrap a double thickness of baking paper around a 1.25 litre (44 fl oz/5 cups) soufflé dish extending 3 cm (1¼ inches) above the rim, then tie with string. Brush with melted butter and sprinkle 1 tablespoon of the sugar into the dish. Shake the dish to coat the base and side evenly.

2 Melt the butter in a saucepan, add the flour and stir over low heat for 2 minutes, or until lightly golden. Add the milk gradually, stirring until smooth. Stir over medium heat until the mixture boils and thickens. Boil for a further minute, then remove from the heat. Transfer to a bowl.

3 Dissolve the coffee in 1 tablespoon of hot water. Add to the milk with the remaining sugar, melted chocolate and egg yolks, then beat until smooth.

4 Beat the egg whites in a clean, dry bowl until stiff peaks form. Fold a little into the chocolate mixture to loosen it slightly. Gently fold in the remaining egg white, then spoon the mixture into the soufflé dish and bake for 40 minutes, or until well risen and just firm. Remove the collar, dust the soufflé with icing sugar and serve.

Chocolate Pear Pancake

serves 2-4

1 large pear
40 g (1¹/2 oz) unsalted butter
1 teaspoon ground cinnamon
1 tablespoon soft brown sugar
1 tablespoon caster (superfine) sugar
3 eggs, separated
2 teaspoons caster (superfine) sugar, extra
30 g (1 oz/¹/4 cup) self-raising flour
1 tablespoon unsweetened cocoa powder
60 ml (2 fl oz/¹/4 cup) milk

1   Peel and quarter the pear. Remove the core and thinly slice.

2   Combine the butter, cinnamon and sugars in a 16 cm (6¹/4 inch) non-stick frying pan. Stir over medium heat until the butter has melted and sugar has dissolved. Add the pear slices, arranging them in an overlapping pattern around the base of the pan. Simmer for 1–2 minutes, or until the pear is just tender. Remove from the heat.

3   Using electric beaters, beat the egg whites until soft peaks form. Gradually add the extra sugar and beat until combined. In a separate bowl, beat the egg yolks, sifted flour and cocoa and milk until smooth. Using a metal spoon, fold in the egg whites. Stir to combine.

4   Return the pan to the heat. Gently pour the pancake mixture over the pears. Cook over low heat for 3–4 minutes, or until the mixture begins to rise. Remove the pan from the heat and put under a hot grill (broiler). Cook for 1–2 minutes or until just browned. Turn the pancake onto a plate and cut into wedges to serve.

White Chocolate Mousse with Almond Biscuits

Serves 8

6 egg yolks

55 g (2 oz/^{1}/4 cup) caster (superfine) sugar

375 ml (13 fl oz/1^1/2 cups) milk

225 g (8 oz/1^1/2 cups) chopped white chocolate

80 ml (2^1/2 fl oz/^{1}/3 cup) cognac

2 teaspoons powdered gelatine

450 ml (16 fl oz) cream (whipping)

unsweetened cocoa powder, for dusting

ALMOND BISCUITS (COOKIES)

1 tablespoon liquid glucose

30 g (1 oz) unsalted butter

1^1/2 tablespoons caster (superfine) sugar

40 g (1^1/2 oz/^{1}/3 cup) plain (all-purpose) flour

30 g (1 oz/^{1}/4 cup) finely chopped blanched almonds

1   Beat the egg yolks and caster sugar in a heatproof bowl until smooth
    and pale. Pour the milk into a saucepan and heat until it is just below
    boiling point. Whisk the hot milk into the egg yolk mixture, then
    return the mixture to the saucepan. Cook over low heat, stirring
    constantly, for about 2 minutes, or until thick. Do not allow the
    mixture to boil.

2   Strain the mixture into a bowl, add the white chocolate and stir until
    the chocolate has melted. Stir in the cognac. Sprinkle the gelatine
    over 1^1/2 tablespoons of cold water in a small heatproof bowl. Set the

bowl in a larger bowl of boiling water and stir until the gelatine has dissolved. Stir the gelatine mixture into the chocolate mixture and set aside to cool for at least 1 hour.

3   Whip the cream until soft peaks form. Using a metal spoon, fold a large scoop of cream into the chocolate mixture, then gently fold in the remaining cream. Divide the mixture among eight 185 ml (6 fl oz/3/4 cup) ramekins and refrigerate until set.

4   Meanwhile, to make the almond biscuits, preheat the oven to 180°C (350°F/Gas 4). Line a baking tray with baking paper. Put the glucose, butter and sugar in a saucepan and cook over low heat, stirring until melted. Increase the heat and bring to the boil. Remove the saucepan from the heat and stir in the flour and almonds.

5   Using half the mixture, spoon 6 teaspoons onto the prepared tray, allowing room for spreading. Bake for 4–5 minutes, or until golden brown. Set aside to cool for 15–20 seconds. Using a spatula and working quickly, lift the biscuits and drape them over a rolling pin or the handle of a wooden spoon. The biscuits will quickly set in a folded shape. Repeat with the remaining mixture. Allow to cool. Lightly dust the mousse with cocoa powder and serve each with two almond biscuits.

Crème Caramel

Serves 8

185 g (6¹/₂ oz/³/₄ cup) sugar

CUSTARD
750 ml (26 fl oz/3 cups) milk
90 g (3¹/₄ oz/¹/₃ cup) caster (superfine) sugar
4 eggs
1 teaspoon natural vanilla extract

1   Preheat the oven to 160°C (315°F/Gas 2–3). Lightly grease eight
    125 ml (4 fl oz/¹/₂ cup) ramekins or moulds.

2   Put the sugar and 60 ml (2 fl oz/¹/₄ cup) of water in a saucepan.
    Stir over low heat until the sugar dissolves. Bring to the boil,
    reduce the heat and simmer until the mixture turns golden and
    starts to caramelize. Remove from the heat and pour enough hot
    caramel into each ramekin to cover the base.

3   To make the custard, heat the milk in a saucepan over low heat until
    almost boiling. Remove from the heat. Whisk together the sugar, eggs
    and vanilla extract for 2 minutes, then stir in the warm milk. Strain
    the mixture into a jug and pour into the ramekins.

4   Put the ramekins in a baking dish and pour in enough boiling water
    to come halfway up the sides of the ramekins. Bake for 30 minutes,
    or until the custard is set. Allow to cool, then refrigerate for at least
    2 hours, or until set.

5   To unmould, run a knife carefully around the edge of each custard
    and gently upturn onto serving plates.

Chocolate Coffee Cups

Makes 20

125 g (4¹/2 oz) dark chocolate melts
20 foil confectionery cases
50 g (1³/4 oz) white chocolate, chopped
1 tablespoon cream (whipping)
1 tablespoon Tia Maria, optional
20 coffee beans

1 Put the dark chocolate melts in a small heatproof bowl and set over a saucepan of simmering water. Stir until the chocolate has melted and is smooth. Cool slightly.

2 Working on one at a time, pour a teaspoon of the chocolate into each confectionery case. Use a small paintbrush to coat the inside with chocolate, making sure the chocolate is thick and there are no gaps. Turn the cases upside down onto a wire rack until the chocolate coating is firm. Set the remaining chocolate aside.

3 Combine the white chocolate, cream and Tia Maria in a small heatproof bowl and set over a saucepan of simmering water. Stir until melted and smooth. Cool slightly, then spoon into the chocolate cases. Put a coffee bean into each cup.

4 Reheat the remaining dark chocolate until melted. Spoon a little dark chocolate over the white chocolate to cover. Tap each cup gently until the surface is level. Allow to set before serving.

Rich Chocolate Sauce Coffee Sauce Carame

Sauces

Sauce Mocha Sauce White Chocolate Sauce

Rich Chocolate Sauce

80 g (2³/4 oz) good-quality dark chocolate, chopped

125 ml (4 fl oz/¹/2 cup) cream (whipping)

1 Put the chocolate and cream in a heatproof bowl and set over a saucepan of simmering water. Stir until chocolate has melted and the mixture is well combined.

 Serve warm with cakes, puddings, waffles, pancakes or ice cream.

Caramel Sauce

150 g (5^1/$_2$ oz) unsalted butter
230 g (7^1/$_2$ oz/1^3/$_4$ cups) soft brown sugar
80 ml (2^3/$_4$ fl oz/^{1}/$_3$ cup) golden or maple syrup
185 ml (6 fl oz/^{3}/$_4$ cup) cream (whipping)

1 Stir all the ingredients in a saucepan over low heat until the sugar has dissolved. Simmer, uncovered, for about 3 minutes, or until thickened slightly.

 Serve warm with cakes, puddings, waffles, pancakes or ice cream.

Coffee Sauce

3 egg yolks

2 tablespoons soft brown sugar

$^1/_2$ teaspoon cornflour (cornstarch)

170 ml (5$^1/_2$ fl oz/$^2/_3$ cup) milk

2 tablespoons instant coffee powder

60 ml (2 fl oz/$^1/_4$ cup) cream (whipping), lightly whipped

1 Whisk the egg yolks, sugar and cornflour in a heatproof bowl until thick. Heat the milk and coffee in a saucepan until almost boiling. Strain through a fine sieve. Gradually whisk into the egg mixture. Return the mixture to the saucepan and stir over low heat until thick. Allow to cool. Stir in the cream.

Serve warm with cakes, puddings, waffles, pancakes or ice cream.

Chocolate Fudge Sauce

150 g (5½ oz/1 cup) chopped dark chocolate

30 g (1 oz) unsalted butter

2 tablespoons golden syrup or dark corn syrup

150 ml (5 fl oz) cream (whipping)

1 Combine the dark chocolate, butter, golden syrup and cream in a saucepan. Heat until the chocolate has melted and the mixture is smooth. Stir until the mixture almost reaches boiling point, then remove from the heat.

 Serve warm with cakes, puddings, waffles, pancakes or ice cream.

Caramel Bar Sauce

4 Snickers bars, or other chocolate, caramel and peanut bars
60 ml (2 fl oz/1/4 cup) milk
185 ml (6 fl oz/3/4 cup) cream (whipping)
100 g (31/2 oz) milk chocolate, chopped

1 Chop the bars and put them in a saucepan with the milk and cream. Stir over low heat until melted. Add the chocolate and stir until melted. Cool to room temperature.

 Serve with vanilla ice cream.

Dark Chocolate Sauce

110 g (3³/4 oz) dark chocolate, chopped
60 g (2¹/4 oz) unsalted butter, cubed

1 Put the dark chocolate and butter in a small heatproof bowl and set the bowl over a small saucepan of simmering water. Stir until the chocolate and butter have melted and the mixture is smooth. Remove from the heat and continue to stir until the sauce is cool and glossy. Serve warm, as the sauce will continue to thicken as it cools.

 Serve warm with cakes, puddings, waffles, pancakes or ice cream.

Mocha Sauce

50 g (1³/4 oz) unsalted butter

150 g (5¹/2 oz) dark chocolate, chopped

375 ml (13 fl oz/1¹/2 cups) cream (whipping)

1 tablespoon instant coffee powder

1–2 tablespoons crème de cacao

1 Combine the butter, chocolate, cream and coffee powder in a small saucepan. Stir over low heat until the butter and chocolate have melted and the mixture is smooth. Add the crème de cacao. Stir until well combined.

 Serve warm with cakes, puddings, waffles, pancakes or ice cream.

Chocolate Liqueur Sauce

170 g (6 oz/³/4 cup) caster (superfine) sugar
60 ml (2 fl oz/¹/4 cup) chocolate liqueur

1. Combine the sugar, liqueur and 185 ml (6 fl oz/³/4 cup) of water in a small saucepan. Stir constantly over low heat until the mixture boils and the sugar has dissolved. Reduce the heat. Simmer without stirring until the mixture begins to thicken and the liquid is reduced by half.

Serve warm with cakes, puddings, waffles, pancakes or ice cream.

Caramel Rum Sauce

225 g (8 oz/1 cup) caster (superfine) sugar
200 ml (7 fl oz) thick (double/heavy) cream
45 g (1½ oz) butter
2 tablespoons dark rum

1 Put the sugar and 150 ml (5 fl oz) water in a saucepan and stir until sugar is dissolved. Bring to the boil and continue to boil until golden brown. Remove from the heat and add the cream. Stir to combine. Add the butter and rum. Stir until smooth.

 Serve warm with cakes, puddings, waffles, pancakes or ice cream.

White Chocolate Sauce

125 g (4¹/₂ oz) good-quality white chocolate, chopped
80 ml (2¹/₂ fl oz/¹/₃ cup) cream (whipping)

1 Put the white chocolate and cream in a small heatproof bowl and set over a small saucepan of simmering water. Stir until melted and smooth.

Serve warm with cakes, puddings, waffles, pancakes or ice cream.

Coffee Cream Sauce

60 g (2¼ oz/¼ cup) caster (superfine) sugar
95 g (3¼ oz/½ cup) soft brown sugar
250 ml (9 fl oz/1 cup) cream (whipping)
30 g (1 oz) instant coffee powder
2 tablespoons Tia Maria (optional)

1 Combine the sugars, cream and coffee in a small saucepan. Stir over medium heat, without boiling, until the sugars have completely dissolved. Bring to the boil, reduce the heat, and simmer, uncovered, for about 3 minutes, or until the mixture has thickened slightly. Stir in the Tia Maria, if using.

Serve warm with cakes, puddings, waffles, pancakes or ice cream.

Chocolate Chilli Sauce

250 g (9 oz) dark chocolate, roughly chopped

250 ml (9 fl oz/1 cup) cream (whipping)

30 g (1 oz) unsalted butter

1 teaspoon chilli powder

1 Combine the chocolate, cream, butter and chilli powder in a saucepan. Cook over very low heat until all the chocolate has melted and the mixture is smooth.

 Serve warm or cold with fresh fruit, profiteroles, ice cream or waffles.

Milk Chocolate and Frangelico Sauce

100 g (3$^{1}/_{2}$ oz/$^{2}/_{3}$ cup) milk chocolate, chopped

60 ml (2 fl oz/$^{1}/_{4}$ cup) thick (double/heavy) cream

2 tablespoons Frangelico

1 Put the chocolate and cream in a small heatproof bowl and set over a small saucepan of simmering water. Stir frequently until the chocolate and cream have melted and the mixture is smooth. Remove from the heat. Stir in the Frangelico and stir until combined.

 Serve warm with cakes, puddings, waffles, pancakes or ice cream.

Chocolate and Baileys Sauce

100 g (3¹/₂ oz/²/₃ cup) dark chocolate, chopped

30 g (1 oz) unsalted butter

60 ml (2 fl oz/¹/₄ cup) Irish cream liqueur, such as Baileys

185 ml (6 fl oz/³/₄ cup) thickened (whipping) cream

1 Put the chocolate, butter, Baileys, and cream in a heatproof bowl and set over a saucepan of simmering water. Stir until the chocolate has melted.

Serve warm with cakes, puddings, waffles, pancakes or ice cream.

index